AmericanHeritage®

AMERICAN VOICES

WORLD WARS AND THE MODERN AGE

Also in the American Heritage® American Voices Series

Colonies and Revolution

Westward Expansion

Civil War and Reconstruction

AmericanHeritage®
AMERICAN VOICES

World Wars and the Modern Age

David C. King

WILEY

John Wiley & Sons, Inc.

Published by John Wiley & Sons, Inc., Hoboken, New Jersey
Published simultaneously in Canada

Design and production by Navta Associates, Inc.

American Heritage is a registered trademark of American Heritage Inc. Its use is pursuant to a license agreement.

For general information about our other products and services, please contact our Customer Care Department within the United States at (800) 762-2974, outside the United States at (317) 572-3993 or fax (317) 572-4002.

Wiley also publishes its books in a variety of electronic formats. Some content that appears in print may not be available in electronic books. For more information about Wiley products, visit our web site at www.wiley.com.

Library of Congress Cataloging-in-Publication Data:

King, David C.
World wars and the modern age / [compiled by] David C. King.
    p. cm.—(American heritage, American voices)
  Includes bibliographical references and index.
  ISBN 0-471-44392-1 (pbk. : acid-free paper)
1. United States—History—1865—Sources—Juvenile literature.   2. United States—Biography—Juvenile literature.
I. King, David C.   II. Series.
  E661.W67   2004
  973—dc22   2004004216

Printed in the United States of America
10 9 8 7 6 5 4 3 2 1

CONTENTS

Introduction to the **AmericanHeritage**®
American Voices Series

For more than four hundred years of our nation's history, Americans have left a long paper trail of diaries, letters, journals, and other personal writings. Throughout this amazingly vast collection, we can often find intriguing information about the events that make up that history. A diary entry, for example, can help us feel we are on the scene, as in this army officer's entry on the eve of a critical Revolutionary War battle: "It is fearfully cold, and a storm setting in. The wind is northeast and beats in the faces of the men. It will be a terrible night for the soldiers who have no shoes."

First-hand accounts can also give us the human side of factual information, such as the service of women in the military during World War I. A text account will describe the women's typical duties and how many served in each branch of service, but a letter from a "lady Marine" to her boyfriend brings it to life when she writes: "Bill, I soon learned I wasn't going to shoot any Huns [Germans]. . . . But we wear the uniform and wear it with pride. We know that each of us makes it possible for a male Marine with an itchy trigger finger to go over there and start shooting." And primary sources can take us inside the minds of those involved in events. These insights are often surprising, as in Eleanor Roosevelt's confession, "I was often terrified by the notion that I would never amount to anything and that I was so homely that no man would want to marry me."

Intriguing fragments like these make up our nation's history. Journals, letters, diaries, and other firsthand accounts are called primary sources. In addition to letters and journals, other voices from the past emerge from newspapers, books, and magazines, from poems and songs, from advertisements, pamphlets, and government documents. Added to the written records are "visual documents" such as sketches, diagrams, patent designs, maps, paintings, engravings, and photographs.

Historians have the fascinating work of sifting through these fragments, searching for the ones that will add a special touch to their reconstruction of the past. But historians are not the only ones who can appreciate these details. America's huge storehouse of primary materials offers a great opportunity to make history more interesting, exciting, and meaningful to everyone. History textbooks are useful for providing the bare bones of history, but firsthand accounts add the muscle and sinew, fleshing out the story with the experiences of real men and women. Primary sources also let you come to your own conclusions about what happened in the past, and they help you make connections between the past and the present.

In creating this series, we've looked for selections that draw out the drama, excitement, tragedy, and humor that have characterized the American experience. The cast of characters comes from a variety of backgrounds and time periods, but they all have authentic American voices, and they have all contributed to our nation's story. We have kept most of the selections short in order to include as many different voices and viewpoints as possible.

The language of primary sources can be difficult. For this series, we have modernized some of the spelling and grammar so that the texts are easier to understand, while being careful to maintain the meaning and tone of the original. We have also provided vocabulary and background information in the margins to help you understand the texts. For the most part, however, we have let the American voices speak for themselves. We hope that what they have to say will interest you, sometimes surprise you, and even inspire you to learn more about America's history.

Introduction to
World Wars and the Modern Age

In a remarkably short period—from about 1870 to 1950—the United States experienced a series of incredible changes. In fact, there never was a period in human history when so much changed in such a short time. A host of inventions led the way in transforming daily life—inventions that included the telephone (1876), the electric light (1879), the recording of sound (1876), electric power to homes and work places (1882), the automobile (1890s), the airplane (1903), motion pictures (1895), radio broadcasting (1920), and television (1930s).

To illustrate this era, I'll use the lifetime of one American, the novelist Willa Cather, whose life spanned nearly all of these years. When Willa Cather was growing up on the Nebraska frontier in the 1870s, many pioneer families still lived in sod houses. Everyone traveled by horse-drawn wagon or carriage; they heated their homes with coal- or wood-burning stoves and used kerosene lanterns for light; they washed with a basin and pitcher because only a few wealthy families had indoor plumbing.

Over her seventy-four years of life, Willa Cather saw the United States change from a nation of farms and small towns to one of huge industries and sprawling cities. Willa Cather was born into a nation of about thirty-eight million people scattered among thirty-seven states. Over the next seventy years eleven new states entered the Union and the population grew by more than one hundred million people. During that time, the percentage of the population engaged in farming dropped from 75 to less than 10 percent.

That span of seventy years also saw America's position in the world greatly changed. In the 1870s, for instance, Great Britain, France, and Germany were the great powers of the world in economic and military terms. By the early 1900s, U.S. industries were producing huge amounts of manufactured goods, and the nation's farms were selling food to countries throughout the world. This abundance gave Americans the world's highest standard of living. Americans were living longer, eating healthier diets, and receiving better health care than people anywhere in the world. In addition, two world wars devastated the once great powers of Europe. The United States emerged from the wars as the world's most powerful nation with the awesome responsibilities of world leadership.

While the years from 1870 to 1950 represented remarkable progress, the forces of change often caused upheaval in people's lives. The process of industrialization created material comfort, for example, but thousands of factory workers found themselves at the mercy of the new economic system. Countless families worked long hours for low pay and could not seem to escape slum housing. Years of struggle ensued before labor unions managed to improve conditions for workers, and popular pressure forced the government to take actions that would protect people's welfare.

The readings in this book include the diaries, letters, and other writings of people who lived during this remarkable era of change and growth. You'll discover that people had trouble adjusting to strange new devices like the telephone and the automobile. You'll share the hopes and fears of a young Russian girl's first days in the United States. You'll also read a young soldier's account of going "over the top" during the grim trench warfare of World War I, and, barely twenty years later, an eyewitness account of the surprise Japanese attack on Pearl Harbor that plunged the United States into World War II. Find out what real Americans, from the super rich "Robber Barons" to Dust Bowl refugees, thought about war, the Depression, jazz, big business, sports, and much more that happened during this amazing period of change.

PART I

A Nation in Transition

Beginning in the 1870s dozens of new industries were propelling the United States into the new age of factories and cities. Many of these industries were spawned by new inventions, such as Alexander Graham Bell's telephone and Thomas Alva Edison's electric light. These developments added the kinds of comfort and convenience to American life that made the nation the envy of the world. By 1900, most families in the fast-growing middle class lived in substantial homes with indoor plumbing, electric lights, a telephone, a private carriage, and two or three servants.

This age of change also had some rough edges. Small shops were replaced by enormous factories that employed hundreds or even thousands of workers. These laborers, along with miners and many farmers, were now at the mercy of huge economic forces. Many found themselves working long hours for very low incomes. At the same time, cities were growing so large and so fast that basic services like water, sewage, and garbage disposal broke down.

In this part you'll read about the drama and excitement of these years of growth and change, and both the positive and negative impacts these changes had on people's lives.

The Centennial Exhibition

In 1876 the American people celebrated the nation's Centennial—the one hundredth anniversary of the Declaration of Independence. A grand Centennial Exhibition was held in Philadelphia from May to November. More than ten million people came to see displays of U.S. achievements in agriculture, crafts, and industry, as well as exhibits from twenty other countries. The exhibition showed that the United States was clearly a country in transition. While the nation was still characterized by family farms and small towns, visitors were most impressed by U.S. progress in industry.

A symbol of the nation's emerging industrial might was the huge Corliss engine, by far the most popular exhibit. The Corliss was the largest steam engine ever made: 700 tons of beautifully polished steel and brass, made with such precision that it powered all the machines in Machinery Hall with only a whisper of sound. The engine was used for the opening day ceremonies, with the inventor George Corliss directing President Ulysses S. Grant and the guest of honor, Dom Pedro, the emperor of Brazil, on how to start the machine. A famous author, William Dean Howells, describes the event and the engine in the following selection.

The Corliss engine, from a drawing made for Harper's Weekly, *May 27, 1876.*

COURTESY, LIBRARY OF CONGRESS

FROM

The Atlantic Monthly

JULY 1876

Mr. Corliss . . . stationed the President at the left throttle-valve and the Emperor at the right. . . . "Are you both ready? Then your majesty will turn the handle." A sound of the rush of steam; the great beam is seen to move. "Now, Mr. President, yours." The sound of steam is multiplied, and the other half of the engine joins in the work. Soon . . . every machine in the Hall hums into action, the sounds of planing, drilling, stamping, turning, and the whir of wheels make a chorus to the murmur of the gear of the underground steam shaft—and the opening ceremonies are complete. . . .

The Corliss engine does not lend itself to description; its personal acquaintance must be sought by those who would understand its vast and almost silent grandeur. . . . In the midst of this incredibly powerful mechanism is a chair where the engineer sits reading his newspaper. Now and then he lays down his paper and clambers up one of the stairways that cover the framework, and touches some irritated spot on the giant's body with a drop of oil, and goes down again and takes up his newspaper.

Alexander Graham Bell's Telephone

While people were impressed by the wondrous age of machines that was emerging, they sometimes had trouble figuring out how a new invention could be used. Alexander Graham Bell's invention of the telephone is a good example. He had received his patent a few weeks before the Centennial opened, and he demonstrated it several times at the exhibition, but no one could understand how to use it. When Emperor Dom Pedro tried it, he was so stunned he dropped the receiver with the exclamation, "Good Lord! It talks!"

About two years after the Centennial, a train wreck near Boston created an emergency in which a telephone proved valuable in getting assistance quickly. This helped people to see the value of voice communication over a distance and, when it became clear that installing telephones and wiring in homes and offices was not impossibly expensive, telephone use grew steadily and rapidly. By 1900 there were more than one million telephones in use, and the numbers never stopped increasing.

The problem with the telephone was that people thought it would work like the telegraph. They wondered how it would be any faster to go to a telephone office and have the operator call in a message to another office, where the message would be written down. No one thought in terms of having a telephone in one's office or home. When Bell offered to sell the invention to Western Union, the major telegraph company at that time, for $100,000, the company president turned him down. "What possible use can we make of an electrical toy?" he asked. In the following reading, a reporter makes some guesses about using the device.

FROM

"The Tele-phone," New York Tribune

NOVEMBER 4, 1876

The Centennial Exhibition has afforded the opportunity to bring into public view many inventions and improvements which otherwise would only have been known to the smaller circles. . . . The tele-phone is a curious device that might fairly find place in the magic of Arabian Tales. Of what use is such an invention? Well, there may be occasions of state when it is necessary for officials who are far apart to talk with each other without the interference of a [telegraph] operator. Or some lover might wish to pop the question directly into the ear of a lady and hear for himself her reply, though miles away; it is not for us to guess how courtships will be carried on in the Twentieth Century.

Thomas Edison's Phonograph

Thomas Alva Edison was scarcely noticed at the Centennial Exhibition, but he was about to burst on the world scene as history's most amazing inventor, with 1,093 patents to his name. He had made important improvements in the telegraph and in stock ticker-tape machines, but the invention that made him world famous as the "Wizard of Menlo Park" was the phonograph.

Until Edison, no one had ever dreamed that sound could be preserved and reproduced. Edison discovered the basic idea almost by accident. He was trying to see if a needle, attached to a telegraph key, could make indentations on a sheet of paper that would be a record of a dot-and-dash telegraph message. Once, when passing a sheet of paper under the moving needle of this "telegraph repeater," Edison and an assistant thought they detected a sound. On the basis of that clue, Edison spent months in trial-and-error experimenting until, by late 1877, he had a small cylinder device, which he called a phonograph. Rarely has an invention caused such instantaneous amazement, as you'll see in the next selection. Edison took his invention to the offices of *Scientific American* and placed his device on the desk of the editor without saying what it was.

FROM

F. C. Beach, Scientific American

DECEMBER 1877

As there was a long shaft having a heavy wheel at one end and a small handle at the other, naturally I gave the handle a twist, and, to my astonishment, the unmistakable words, emitted from a kind of telephone mouthpiece, broke out, "Good morning! What do you think of the phonograph?"

To say that I was astonished is a poor way of expressing my first impressions, and Edison appeared to enjoy his little joke on me immensely. Like a flash the news went among the staff that Edison had brought in a machine which could talk, and soon there was an excited crowd around my desk. . . . Edison was kept going for two or three hours, but at last the crowd attained such proportions that I feared the floor would give way under the abnormal weight, and I requested the inventor to stop.

The Phonograph Craze

News of Edison's "Machine that Talks" swept the nation, and within a year five hundred "phonograph parlors" were in operation throughout the country. People came from miles around to pay a few pennies to hear the device and have the chance to talk into it. But the phonograph craze could not last long. The machines were far from perfect, and the aluminum foil covering the cylinder gradually wore out. In addition, once people had their curiosity satisfied, there was no need to go back. Edison, too, lost interest, because he had become absorbed by a new problem—the electric light. Ten years passed before Edison returned to the phonograph. He and others soon made the needed improvements that turned the phonograph and records into big business.

Edison and Electric Lights

Inventors had been trying to create electric lighting throughout the 1800s. One major problem was finding a way to subdivide electric current into small units that could be used in a house or business. An 1878 British government report concluded that "the problem of subdividing electrical current cannot be solved by the human brain." Edison solved that problem by creating a "glow lamp," an incandescent lamp with a rod that would glow without burning up. The next problem was finding a substance for that rod, or filament. In 1879, after literally hundreds of experiments, he found that a tiny piece of carbonized bamboo would glow for many hours.

While Edison's electric light was considered a miracle, his greatest achievement may have been his system for lighting an entire neighborhood in New York City. He and his assistants had to invent everything from scratch: light sockets, lamps, switches, plugs, insulated wire, meters to measure the amount of electricity used, and generators to produce electrical power and distribute it. The following selection is a reporter's description of the first electric lighting in the Pearl Street area of New York City, where the *New York Times* offices were located.

FROM

The New York Times

SEPTEMBER 5, 1882

It was not until about seven o'clock, when it began to grow dark, that the electric light really made itself known and showed how bright and steady it is. Then the twenty-seven electric lamps in the [*New York Times*] editorial rooms . . . made those [rooms] as bright as day, but without any unpleasant glare. It was a light that a man could sit down under and write for hours without the [awareness] of having any artificial light about him. . . . The light was soft, mellow, and grateful to the eye, and it seemed almost like writing by daylight to have a light without a particle of flicker and with scarcely any heat to make the head ache.

The whole lamp looks so much like a gas burner surmounted by a shade that nine people out of ten would not have known the rooms were lighted by electricity except that the light was more brilliant than gas and a hundred times steadier. To turn on the light nothing is required but to turn the thumbscrew, no matches are needed. . . . As soon as it is dark enough to need artificial light, you turn the thumbscrew and the light is there; no nauseous smell, no flicker, no glare.

Farming Becomes a Business

The development of machinery also had a great impact on farming. Earlier in the nation's history, most farms produced enough food to meet their owners' needs, with some left over to sell or trade. In the late 1800s, machinery enabled farmers to cultivate much larger acreage of a single cash crop, such as wheat, cotton, or corn. Sales of the harvest provided the money needed to support the family, to buy a few luxury items on

The Risks of One-Crop Farming

When times were good, the cash-crop farmers prospered. This form of agriculture, however, presented two great risks. First, if the weather or insects destroyed a crop, the farm family had nothing to fall back on, and they still had to pay loans used to buy equipment or more land. (In diversified farming, it was rare for a family to lose all its crops and its farm animals.) The second risk was that, if all farmers had a great crop year, there would be too much wheat (or corn, cotton, or sugar) on the market. This would force the price down, often to disastrous levels.

occasion, and to pay for more land and the expensive machinery. Farming became another form of business.

In the following selection, Hamlin Garland describes wheat farming on the Great Plains.

FROM

Hamlin Garland's A Son of the Middle Border

1914

As I look back over my life . . . the song of the reaper fills a large place in my mind. We were all worshipers of wheat in those days. The men thought and talked of little else between seeding and harvest. . . .

We trembled when the storm lay hard upon the wheat, we exulted as the lilac shadows of noonday drifted over it! We went out into it at noon when all was still—so still we could hear the pulse of the transforming sap as it crept from cool root to swaying plume. We stood before it at evening when the setting sun flooded it with crimson, the bearded heads lazily swirling under the wings of the wind . . . and our hearts expanded with the beauty and the mystery of it—and back of all this was the knowledge that its abundance meant a new carriage, an addition to the house, or a new suit of clothes. . . .

[At harvest time] we got out the reaper, put the sickles in order, and Father laid in a store of provisions. Extra hands were hired, and at last, early on a hot July morning, the boss mounted to his seat on the **self-rake McCormick** and drove into the field. Frank rode the lead horse, four **stalwart** hands and myself took stations behind the reaper, and the battle was on! . . .

The crops on our farm in those first years were enormous, and prices were good; and yet the homes of the neighborhood were slow in taking on grace and comfort. I don't know why this was so, unless it was that the men were continually buying more land and more machinery.

self-rake McCormick: a reaper that cut the wheat *and* raked it into bundles.

stalwart: strong, sturdy.

Coming to a New Land

In the late 1800s, more people than ever before looked to the United States as the land of hope and opportunity. The growth of cities and the development of modern industries added to the image of abundance. Poor families in southern and eastern Europe began to believe that the streets of America were paved with gold. Since they saw little to hope for in their native countries, growing numbers decided to emigrate to the United States.

The result was a remarkable increase in the number of immigrants arriving from Europe. Between 1860 and 1900, more than fourteen million newcomers came, and another eighteen million arrived between 1900 and 1930. These huge numbers helped triple the nation's population from thirty million in 1860 to nearly ninety-two million in 1910.

The new immigrants arrived with a mixture of hope, anxiety, and fear. In the next selection, an Italian immigrant, Edward Corsi, recalls arriving in New York Harbor in the late 1890s.

FROM

Edward Corsi's In the Shadow of Liberty

1935

My first impression of the new world will always remain etched in my memory. . . . The steamer *Florida,* fourteen days out of Naples, filled to capacity with sixteen hundred natives of Italy, had weathered one of the worst storms in our captain's memory; and glad we were . . . to leave the open sea and come at last through the Narrows into the Bay.

My mother, my stepfather, my brother, . . . and my two sisters, . . . all of us together, . . . clustered on the foredeck for fear of separation and looked with wonder on this miraculous land of our dreams. . . .

Passengers all about us were crowding against the rail. Jabbered conversation, sharp cries, laughs and cheers—a

Immigrants in the Midwest and West

While thousands of new arrivals each year stayed in or near New York City, many headed west. The 1910 census revealed that in eight states—Illinois, Michigan, Minnesota, Wisconsin, the Dakotas, Montana, and Utah—at least 50 percent of the population was foreign-born.

steadily rising din filled the air. Mothers and fathers lifted up the babies so that they too could see, off to the left, the Statue of Liberty.

I looked at that statue with a sense of bewilderment, half doubting its reality. Looming shadowy through the mist, it brought silence to the decks. . . . This symbol of America . . . inspired awe in the hopeful immigrants. Many older persons among us, burdened with a thousand memories of what they were leaving behind, had been openly weeping. . . . Now somewhat steadied, I suppose, by . . . the symbol of America's freedom, they dried their tears.

The Statue of Liberty was a gift to the United States from France, America's vital ally in the War for Independence. The 151-foot-high sculpture was the work of Frédéric-Auguste Bartholdi. It was officially dedicated on October 28, 1886. A poem by the Jewish immigrant Emma Lazarus was added later. The poem contained the famous lines

Give me your tired, your poor,
Your huddled masses yearning to breathe free,
The wretched refuse of your teeming shore.
Send these, the homeless, tempest-tost to me,
I lift my lamp beside the golden door!

Andrew Carnegie: An Immigrant's Success Story

Andrew Carnegie came to the United States as a penniless immigrant from Scotland in 1848. By the late 1800s, he owned a steel-manufacturing company that became one of the United States's giant corporations. After amassing a personal fortune estimated at $450 million, he left the business and devoted the rest of his life to giving the money away. His wealth financed the building of several colleges, dozens of small-town libraries, concert halls, and peace organizations.

In the following reading, Carnegie describes his first experience with capitalistic investment—investing money in a business and sharing in any profits from the business. He was working for a railroad company at the time and his boss offered him a chance to buy ten shares of the company stock if he could come up with the purchase price of five hundred dollars.

FROM

Andrew Carnegie's Gospel of Wealth

1 9 0 0

Here was a queer position. The available assets of the whole family were not five hundred dollars. But there was one member of the family whose ability, pluck and resource never failed us. I felt sure the money could be raised somehow or other by my mother.

The matter was laid before the council of three that night, and the oracle [his mother] spoke: "Must be done. Mortgage our house. I will take the steamer in the morning for Ohio and see Uncle and ask him to arrange it. I am sure he can." This was done. Of course her visit was successful—where did she ever fail?

The money was procured, paid over; ten shares of Adams Express Company stock was mine; but no one knew our little home had been mortgaged "to give our boy a start."

Adams Express stock then paid monthly dividends of one per cent, and the first check for five dollars arrived. . . .

The next day being Sunday, we boys—myself and my ever-constant companions—took our usual Sunday afternoon stroll in the country, and sitting down in the woods, I showed them this check.

Here was something new to all of us, for none of us had ever received anything but from toil. A return from capital was something strange and new.

How money could make money, how, without any attention from me, this mysterious golden visitor should come, led to much speculation upon the part of the young fellows; and I was for the first time hailed as a "capitalist."

Mary Antin

Beginning about 1880, thousands of Jews chose to flee their homes in Russia and Russian-controlled Poland because of the prejudice and hatred they encountered. The development of fairly inexpensive railroad and steamship fares made it possible for them to dream of starting a new life in the United States. The largest number of Jews went to New York City—a total of five hundred thousand between 1880 and 1900—but the Antin family went to Boston in 1894. Twelve-year-old Mary was fascinated by everything in this new world of the United States, and not long after her arrival, she decided she would become a writer in order to describe her experiences. She became a well-known author, and her first book, *The Promised Land,* is still widely read.

FROM

Mary Antin's The Promised Land

1912

Our initiation into American ways began with the first step on the new soil. My father found occasion to instruct or correct us even on the way from the pier to Wall Street, which journey we made crowded together in a rickety cab. He told us not to lean out of the windows, not to point, and explained the word **greenhorn**. We did not want to be greenhorns and gave the strictest attention to my father's instructions. . . .

The first meal was an **object lesson** of much variety. My father produced several kinds of food, ready to eat, without any cooking, from little tin cans that had printing all over them. He attempted to introduce us to a queer, slippery kind of fruit which he called banana, but had to give it up for the time being. After the meal he had better luck with a

greenhorn: slang for inexperienced.

object lesson: a lesson that includes a demonstration.

curious piece of furniture on runners which he called rocking chair. There were five of us newcomers, and we found five different ways of getting into the American machine of perpetual motion and as many ways of getting out of it. One born and bred to the use of a rocking chair cannot imagine how **ludicrous** people can make themselves when attempting to use it for the first time. We laughed . . . over our various experiments with the novelty, which was a wholesome way of letting off steam after the unusual excitement of the day.

In our **flat** we did not think of such a thing as storing the coal in the bathtub. There was no bathtub. So in the evening of the first day my father conducted us to the **public baths.** As we moved along in a little procession, I was delighted with the illumination of the streets. So many lamps, and they burned until morning, my father said, and so people did not need to carry lanterns. In America, then, everything was free, as we had heard in Russia. Light was free; the streets were as bright as a synagogue on a holy day. Music was free; we had been serenaded by a brass band of many pieces soon after our installation on Union Place.

Education was free. That subject my father had written about repeatedly, as comprising his chief hope for us children, the essence of American opportunity, the treasure that no thief could touch, not even misfortune or poverty. It was the one thing that he was able to promise us when he sent for us; surer, safer than bread or shelter. On our second day I was thrilled with the realization of what this freedom of education meant. A little girl from across the alley came and offered to conduct us to school. My father was out, but we five between us had a few words of English by this time. We knew the word school. We understood. This child, who had never seen us till yesterday . . . was able to offer us the freedom of the schools of Boston! No application made, no questions asked, no examinations, rulings, exclusions; . . . no fees. The doors stood open. The smallest child could show us the way.

ludicrous: ridiculous.

flat: an apartment.

public baths: By the 1890s, indoor plumbing was becoming almost universal, but in poor sections of major cities several families shared facilities, and often there was no bathtub or shower. Public baths, one for males, another for females, were well supervised and represented a great step forward in city sanitation.

City Magic

Cities and Culture

Cities were the center for art, theater, concerts, and other cultural institutions. In Chicago, for example, the following buildings opened their doors in the thirteen years between 1879 and 1892: the Art Institute, the Chicago Auditorium, the American Conservatory of Music, the Chicago Symphony Hall, the University of Chicago, and the Field Museum.

Frank Sprague: An Unsung Hero

In 1888, Frank Sprague left Thomas Edison's company to try installing electric trolley cars in Richmond, Virginia, using the tracks laid for horsedrawn trolley cars. The quiet speed and efficiency of Sprague's invention was an instant success. Within three years, nearly a hundred cities were installing trolley lines, and many of the lines extended out into the suburbs.

Many people—including immigrants and Americans from farming regions—were attracted to the fast-growing cities. The cities were colorful, busy, exciting places. The first skyscrapers appeared, made possible by advances in engineering as well as the invention of elevators. Trolley cars, electrically powered by overhead wires, whisked people quickly and quietly through crowded streets. In some cities, elevated railroads carried passengers *above* the streets to homes in the outskirts of the city or in suburbs. The bright lights drew people to busy theaters, museums, and concert halls, and by the early 1900s, the first flickering motion pictures.

The reading that follows will give you an idea of what New York City was like at the turn of the century.

FROM

Giuseppe Giacosa's Impressions of America

1908

In New York, toward evening, when the working day ends, miles of carriages scatter the innumerable crowds, which all day long conduct their affairs downtown, to all parts of the upper city. The six parallel elevated railway lines each run trains of five or six enormous coaches every five minutes, all jammed to overflowing with people. . . .

When the train runs at its highest along the level of the top floors, where more light enters, the whole interior equipment and furniture of the house becomes visible. There are pleasant draperies, cloths on the tables, nice curtains, copious and commodious furniture, in general an air of solidity and comfort which in Italy we do not see in our provincial cities, except perhaps for such exceptions as the homes of lawyers, doctors, judges, merchants. These people, be it understood, live by their own day's labor, with salaries of four or even three dollars a day, the ordinary pay of a worker. These are settled people; they neither owe nor are owed; they are not in danger of ruin; and their needs are not limited to that which barely keeps them from dying but also include what is desirable for living.

Amusements and Pastimes

For the first time in America's history, large numbers of people had enough leisure time and money to enjoy a new age of entertainment and sports. People flocked to such entertainments as the Ringling Bros. and Barnum & Bailey Circus (and many cheap imitations), dramatic plays and comedies, and Buffalo Bill's Wild West Show. Spectator sports witnessed an explosive growth, with baseball becoming the national craze. Teams outgrew their ballparks almost as soon as they were built, and overflow crowds often lined the outfield. People were also active in sports, with bicycling being by far the most popular.

Among the greatest pastimes were trips to world's fairs. The largest and most impressive was the Chicago World's Columbian Exposition in 1893, an extravaganza that drew more than twenty-seven million visitors. The following selection is one visitor's account.

A LETTER FROM
The Chicago World's Fair
1893

Dear Paula,

This is the most amazing place, an entire city designed by the nation's greatest architects and adorned by our most famous sculptors. At night, thousands of electric lights make the most wondrous scene I have ever witnessed. They call it the "White City," and all of the buildings are indeed white. One of the most impressive structures is the Manufacturing and Liberal Arts Building. It covers 30 acres and the guide book states that it is the largest building in the world under one roof. . . .

I wish you could see the great wheel designed by a man named George Ferris. It should be one of the Seven Wonders of the World and it shows what American science and industry can do. This giant wheel is 250 feet in diameter, and it holds thirty-six cabins, or cars, each able to hold 40 people. After waiting nearly an hour, I entered one of the cars and 1,440 of us were lifted slowly and gently into the air. The great wheel paused six times in its revolution to give us breathtaking views of Lake Michigan, the exposition grounds, and the entire city.

The interior of the Electricity Building at the Chicago World's Fair, 1893.

The world's first Ferris wheel, 1893.

Big Business and National Markets

The transcontinental railroads, which had first appeared in 1869, had a profound impact on the way Americans conducted business. All sections of the country were now knit together by steel rails. In the past, a company that made oil, food items, or hardware usually sold goods within a short distance of the factory. With the railroads, a business owner could now sell products throughout the country. Not surprisingly, the first nationwide chain of grocery stores was named the Great Atlantic & Pacific Tea Co. (which soon became the A&P).

A few businessmen also recognized that the competition for national markets among dozens of companies kept prices high and profits low. Those who had skill, good luck, and a way to raise money, or capital, began to take control of certain industries. John D. Rockefeller in oil and Andrew Carnegie in steel, for example, began to drive their competitors out of business.

The owners of the nation's giant corporations became known as robber barons because the often ruthless methods they used to build their fortunes were seen as robbing the public. The owners, however, felt quite justified in controlling so much of the nation's economy, as you'll see in the first of the following two readings. The third selection, from a former owner of an oil company, shows the kind of tactics Rockefeller used to cut out the competition.

FROM

Andrew Carnegie's "Wealth"

1889

In the last few hundred years, there has been a revolution. There used to be very little difference between the way of life of a community's leaders and the ordinary people. Now however, there is a tremendous difference between the palace of the millionaire and the cottage of the laborer.

But this change is really a very good thing. In fact, it's absolutely necessary for the progress of humanity, because it is the rich who preserve the best literature and art and the other refinements of civilization.

Here's how to solve the problem of poverty: Don't pass any laws controlling either how businessmen make money or what they do with it. Most of the community's money will then end up in the hands of a few men, but this is all right if these men consider themselves not as owners of the money but merely as temporary keepers of it. Because these men are wise (or they wouldn't be rich) they will be able to make good decisions about how to spend the money to help the community. In fact, their decisions will be better than those of the people of the community themselves.

survival of the fittest: a term coined by the English biologist Charles Darwin to describe how animals that are better fit for their environment will survive and reproduce.

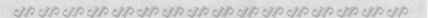

FROM

A Statement by John D. Rockefeller Jr.

1903

The growth of a large business is merely a **survival of the fittest.** The American Beauty rose can be produced in the splendor and fragrance which brings cheer to its beholder only by sacrificing the early buds which grow up around it. This is not an evil tendency in business. It is merely the working-out of a law of nature and a law of God.

A cartoon of Rockefeller's "American Beauty Rose." He's cutting off the competition to produce a blossom called "Standard Oil Co."

Creating Monopoly Power

By 1882, Rockefeller's Standard Oil Company controlled roughly 95 percent of the nation's oil industry. In addition to his often ruthless business practices, he also continually reinvested his profits back into the company. He advised his business partners to "take out what you've got to have to live on, but leave the rest in [the company]. Don't buy new clothes or fast horses; let your wife wear her last year's bonnet." After about 1920, Rockefeller used a large part of his fortune to establish foundations to benefit society.

FROM

George Rice's Testimony

1889

My refinery was forced out of business three years ago by the Standard Oil Trust. They did it partly by using their power to force the railroads to give them lower freight rates than I was able to get.

That was only part of the problem. I could sell my oil at two to three cents a gallon cheaper than Standard Oil and still make a nice profit. But because they were so big, they could afford to go to my customers and offer them oil even below the cost of producing it. Of course, after I was driven out of business, my old customers had to pay whatever Standard Oil demanded.

These kinds of savage attacks clearly show both their power to do evil and the uselessness of trying to fight them.

THE HAROLD SETON COLLECTION OF THE NEW-YORK HISTORICAL SOCIETY

Alva Vanderbilt,
dressed for one of
her famous parties.

Lifestyles of the Super Rich

Between 1870 and 1900, the gap between the poor and the rich grew enormously. The super rich, in that age before the income tax, began to compete with one another in lavish displays of wealth. Large crowds gathered to watch elegantly dressed people arrive at the theater or a society ball, the women wearing gowns costing $5,000 or more. Families like the Astors and the Vanderbilts spent millions building extravagant "cottages"; the Vanderbilts' Newport, Rhode Island, cottage cost $9 million to furnish. The newly rich were often crude in their displays, such as the family that held a banquet for one hundred dogs and their owners, with a meal that included fricasseed dog bones.

The Plight of Workers and Farmers

As industries grew and cities became larger and more crowded, there were few laws or government agencies to protect those who were powerless: the factory workers, miners, and farm families. Factory managers could hire newly arrived immigrants for unskilled work, paying them low wages. Workers who demanded better pay or safer working conditions were simply fired. Men and women who were out of work for any reason, including accident or injury, received no unemployment benefits, medical care, or welfare; these cushions against disaster did not exist in the late 1800s. The result was a decline in the living standards of industrial workers, the urban poor, and many farm families.

The following selection provides a look at the conditions faced by industrial workers. The reading is journalist John Spargo's exposé of child labor.

FROM

John Spargo's The Bitter Cry of the Children

1906

[Spargo's account was based on his visit to a coal mine, where young "breaker boys" were hired to separate slate and rock from the lumps of coal.]

Crouched over the chutes, the boys sit hour after hour, picking out the pieces of slate and other refuse from the coal as it rushes past to the washers. From the cramped position they have to assume most of them become more or less deformed and bent-backed like old men. When a boy has been working for some time and begins to get round-shouldered, his fellows say that "he's got his boy to carry round wherever he goes." The coal is hard, and accidents to the hands, such as cut, broken, or crushed fingers, are common among the boys. Sometimes there is a worse accident; a terrified shriek is heard, and a boy is mangled and torn in the machinery or disappears in the chute to be picked out later, smothered and dead. Clouds of dust . . . are inhaled by the boys, [leading to] asthma and miners' consumption. The gloom . . . appalled me. . . . The harsh grinding roar of the machinery and the ceaseless rushing of coal through the chutes filled the ears. I tried to pick out the pieces of slate from the hurrying stream of coal, often missing them; my hands were bruised and cut in a few minutes; I was covered from head to foot with coal dust and for many hours afterward I was expectorating some of the small particles of anthracite I had swallowed.

I could not do that work and live, but there were boys of ten and twelve years of age doing it for fifty and sixty cents a day. Some of them had never been inside of a school; few of them could read a child's **primer.**

primer: a beginning reader.

COURTESY OF U.S. NATIONAL ARCHIVES AT COLLEGE PARK, MD

"Breaker boys" at a Pennsylvania coal mine, 1911.

Muckrakers: The Power of the Press

A handful of writers played a key role in exposing the conditions in slums, factories, and mines, as well as abuses on the part of business and railroad owners. In the early 1900s, Samuel McClure, the editor of *McClure's Magazine,* brought many of these journalists together and began printing several of their articles in each new issue. The *McClure's* articles caused a sensation and raised public awareness of the problems. In 1906 President Theodore Roosevelt said these writers were like a character in John Bunyan's *Pilgrim's Progress,* who did nothing but rake the muck and filth. These "muckrakers," he said, "are often indispensable to the well-being of society, but only if they know when to stop raking the muck." The nickname "Muckrakers" stuck and the writers accepted it with pride.

Labor Wars

By the 1870s, Americans realized that the individual was helpless against the power of businesses, banks, and railroads. Both workers and farmers tried to gain strength by creating a united front; workers tried to achieve this by forming unions, while farmers turned to social and political action.

In this selection, Samuel Gompers, who helped organize the Cigarmakers International Union of America, describes an early effort to form a union and use a *strike* (a refusal to work) to force owners to improve wages or working conditions. The owners, however, had too much power. They owned the shops, usually in tenements, so they could lock out the workers, evict them from tenement apartments, and blacklist (agree not to hire) leaders of the union.

FROM

Samuel Gompers's Autobiography

1877

We established provision kitchens . . . from which we distributed food and money—chiefly food, which we purchased wholesale. Meat and bread were distributed daily upon presentation of tickets given by the Relief Committee. Once a week we distributed to each family a supply of groceries. To single men we gave tickets for one meal a day. At first we attempted to supply medical assistance, but as the weeks of the strike increased in number, and the pinch of want became very keen, it finally became necessary to diminish and then discontinue even the provision kitchen. . . . More than anything else the strikers were anxious to keep roofs over their heads. On October 24, the employers brought into action a terrible weapon. . . . [They] evicted workers from ten tenements. We had been trying to guard against this . . . by helping with rent payments, but our resources could not keep pace with the demands made on them. . . .

Another . . . factor in our campaign was the factory we undertook to operate. . . . We . . . employed twenty-four hundred workers. The whole project was entered into as a . . . move to get a number of cigarmakers at work. . . .

Just before Christmas . . . a number of firms locked out their workmen who had been the financial backbone of the strike. . . . The cigarmakers were forced to make terms as best they could by groups. The strike slowly crumbled away. . . .

[Several weeks after the strike, Gompers found work at M. Stachelberg & Company.]

I had sat at my bench and had made about twenty cigars when Mr. Stachelberg came . . . over to me, examined the cigars that I had made, said that they were good, and greeted me cordially. But five minutes afterwards the foreman told me . . . that Mr. Stachelberg wanted to see me in his office. On my arrival there he asked me to take a seat. . . . He said that he regretted very much what he was about to say to me, but he could not help it; that he liked me personally and liked my work but that the Manufacturers' Association had decided that the leaders of the strike should not be employed by any member of the Association. He did not want to discharge me, but I would confer a great favor . . . if I would leave.

The Government and Big Business

In the closing decades of the nineteenth century, workers and farmers frequently learned that the state and federal governments would always side with the giant corporations. This lesson was particularly painful for labor unions, because state governors and the president were willing to call out the national guard or the army to put down a strike. Public attitudes began to change at the turn of the century. In the early 1900s, unions gradually won the right to bargain collectively and to strike. They reached the height of their strength from the 1930s through the 1950s, gaining for U.S. workers the highest living standards in the world.

PART II

EXPANSION AND REFORM

The rapid emergence of the United States as an industrial nation contributed to two important changes in the country's story. For the first time the United States was considered one of the world's great economic powers, nearly equal to the established powers like Great Britain and Germany. This new economic position made U.S. businessmen eager to compete with those great powers, especially in opening new markets in Asia, Africa, and Latin America. Some Americans also thought the United States should become a great military power as well. In the 1890s these expansionists, as they were called, found several opportunities to expand the United States's position in world affairs.

A second important change was a movement for reform as people realized the need for government action to correct the problems emerging from the rapid growth of cities and industries. The demand for change, which became known as Progressivism, came from middle-class Americans, not from the factory workers or farm families.

The readings in this section describe both the United States's emergence as a world power and the reforms of the Progressive years.

The Spanish-American War

In April 1898, the United States declared war against Spain because of Spanish actions in Cuba. In the 1500s, Spain had been one of the world's dominant nations, with great wealth from its empire in Central and South America. By the late 1800s there was little left of the wealth or the empire, except for a few island possessions such as Cuba, Puerto Rico, and the Philippines.

The sinking of the U.S. battleship Maine.

In 1895, the Cuban people revolted against Spanish rule, but Spain struck back hard. Under General Valerian Weyler, the Spanish ruthlessly put down the rebellion and forced thousands of Cuban men, women, and children into prison camps. Those events took place at a time when two major newspaper owners—William Randolph Hearst of the *New York Journal* and Joseph Pulitzer of the *New York World*—were locked in a bitter battle for readers. Both men ordered their reporters and artists to play up the brutality of the man they called "Butcher" Weyler. The reporting became increasingly sensational and the American people began calling for intervention by U.S. military forces.

Never before had the press played such a vital role in bringing about war fever. In February 1898, when the U.S. battleship *Maine* blew up in the harbor at Havana, Cuba, Americans readily believed what the *Journal* and *World* said—that the Spanish were responsible. Actually there was no reason for the Spanish to risk bringing the United States into the conflict, nor was there any evidence that the Spanish were responsible. Nevertheless, "Remember the *Maine*" became the U.S. rallying cry.

The following reading presents an account by the artist-reporter Charles J. Post, who found himself so caught up in the desire for war that he left his job to enlist as a private in a New York regiment.

Only 400 Americans were killed in battle in the Spanish-American War, but several thousand died of disease, including dysentery, yellow fever, malaria, and typhoid.

⚜ ⚜ ⚜ ⚜ ⚜ ⚜ ⚜ ⚜ ⚜ ⚜ ⚜ ⚜ ⚜ ⚜ ⚜

FROM

Charles J. Post's Memoirs

1900

When we steamed into the harbor of Havana, we saw the *Maine,* a tangled wreck. We commoner folk began to boil and seethe with ardor to kill a Spaniard. . . . I knew, of course, that Mr. Hearst had **incited** the war and was boosting circulation by inciting patriotism. And I knew, too, that many reporters and artists had filed their reports without ever leaving their hotel rooms in Havana. But there I was, like so many, caught up in the war excitement and now a private in the 71st Infantry Regiment of the New York National Guard. . . .

incited: stirred up feelings for [war].

I don't know who was less prepared for war—the Spaniards or the Americans. We had heavy winter uniforms, no training, and terrible food; the enemy had terrible officers and no will to fight. There was no strategy. The best fighters were the Negro troops who followed Colonel Roosevelt and his Rough Riders up San Juan Hill. . . . It was a brilliant victory . . . against odds and in spite of the blunders. . . .

The 71st was trapped at "Bloody Ford" [a stream crossing], floundering in the water because our general could not decide which way to go. We cheered as Colonel Roosevelt and his Rough Riders pushed past us. "Don't cheer, but fight," the Colonel shouted. "Now's the time to fight!" They rushed up San Juan Hill, seized the fort, and won the war.

Victory in the Philippines

When the war began Theodore Roosevelt was assistant secretary of the navy. Before he resigned to form his volunteer cavalry outfit—the Rough Riders—he ordered Commodore George Dewey, commander of the Pacific fleet, to head for Manila Bay in the Philippines. Eleven days after war was declared, Dewey's fleet steamed into Manila Bay. The steel ships of the U.S. fleet quickly destroyed the wooden ships of the Spanish, and Spain's rule of the Philippines was soon ended. The quick victory was cheered throughout the United States and made people even more eager to send troops to Cuba.

America's Colonial Empire

Following the surprisingly easy victory in the war, the United States was now in control of Spain's former colonies. Expansionist Americans were certain that the United States should take over these colonies. After all, they argued, the great powers of Europe were busily dividing most of Africa and much of Asia into colonies, and a colonial empire was a sign of a truly great power.

Other Americans disagreed. The United States had never before ruled colonies, and the Constitution said nothing about taking over conquered lands. In addition, the people of Cuba and the Philippines had fought alongside the Americans, convinced that the United States would help them gain their independence. How could we now say that the United States was replacing Spain as their rulers?

As the first of the following readings indicates, President William McKinley was uncertain what to do, then finally decided to keep the Philippines as well as Cuba and Puerto Rico. The second reading is Massachusetts senator George Hoar's argument against annexing the Philippines.

Other American Possessions

The United States gained other possessions in the Pacific during the 1890s. The most important acquisition was the Hawaiian Islands where U.S. sugar and pineapple growers had come to dominate the Hawaiian economy. After Americans staged a revolution and took control from native Hawaiians, Congress voted to annex the islands. Both Hawaii and Alaska (purchased from Russia in 1867) were granted statehood in 1959. The United States also gained control of tiny Pacific islands, including Wake Island and Guam. These islands were important as naval bases and as coaling stations for U.S. steamships and warships.

FROM

President McKinley's Recollections

1900

When . . . I realized that the Philippines had dropped into our laps I confess that I did not know what to do with them. . . . I walked the floor of the White House night after night until midnight, and I am not ashamed to tell you gentlemen that I went down on my knees and prayed Almighty God for light and guidance more than one night. And one night it came to me this way . . . that we could not give them back to Spain—that would be cowardly and dishonorable; . . . and there was nothing left for us to do but to take them all and to educate the Filipinos, and uplift and Christianize them, and by God's grace do the best we could for them. . . . And then I went to bed . . . and slept soundly, and the next morning I sent for the chief engineer of the War Department, and I told him to put the Philippines on the map of the United States and there they are and there they will stay while I am President!

FROM

A Speech by Senator George Hoar

1900

I claim that under the Declaration of Independence you can not govern a foreign territory, a foreign people, another people than your own . . . because you think it is for their good, when they do not; because you think you are going to give them the blessings of liberty. You have no right at the cannon's mouth to impose on an unwilling people your Declaration of Independence and your Constitution and your notions of freedom and . . . of what is good.

The Beginning of the Progressive Movement

The middle-class people who became known as progressives included lawyers, doctors, office workers, merchants, writers, and a fast-growing number of women. Both Republicans and Democrats were involved. Many progressives demanded action by all levels of government to improve conditions for industrial workers, end child labor, improve schools, end the monopoly power of giant corporations, and get rid of slums. For others, the reform movement involved a simple desire to help those who were poor, sick, or disabled. Jane Addams, one of the great progressive reformers, wrote, "It is natural to feed the hungry and care for the sick; and it is certainly natural to give pleasure to the young and comfort to the aged."

In 1889, Addams bought a large house in a run-down section of Chicago and turned it into a settlement house—a place run by volunteer social workers where poor families could come for help, education, and enjoyment. The idea of settlement houses originated in England, but it was the model of Addams's Hull House that was soon copied in other cities throughout the United States. The following article summarizes some of the settlement's activities.

FROM
A Journal Article by Jane Addams
1893

It has always been the policy of Hull House to co-operate as much as possible with public institutions. The Chicago Public Library has an almost unique system of branch reading-rooms and library stations. . . . Hull House was made one of these. . . . The City Library supplies English magazines and papers and two librarians who are in charge. There are papers in Italian, German, Bohemian, and French. Hull House gives the room free of rent. The number of readers the first month was 1,213; during the fifth month, 2,454. . . .

Every Thursday evening for three years, save during the three summer months, we have had a lecture of some sort at Hull House. This has come to be an expected event in the neighborhood. . . .

The industrial education of Hull House has always been somewhat limited. From the beginning we have had large and enthusiastic cooking classes. . . . We have also always had sewing, mending, and embroidery classes. This leads me to speak of the children who meet weekly at Hull House, whose organization is between classes and clubs. There are three hundred of them who come on three days. . . .

A nursery at Chicago's Hull House, c. 1900.

New York City's tenements made parts of Manhattan the most densely populated region of the world. In 1900, a state commission reported that more than a million people lived in 43,000 crowded tenements.

A hundred Italian girls come on Monday. They sew and carry home a new garment, which becomes a pattern for the entire family. Tuesday afternoon has always been devoted to school-boys' clubs; they are practically story-telling clubs. The most popular stories are legends and tales of chivalry. The one hundred and fifty little girls on Friday afternoon are not very unlike the boys, although they want to sew while they are hearing their stories. The value of these clubs, I believe, lies almost entirely in their success in arousing the higher imagination. We have had a kindergarten at Hull House ever since we have lived there. . . .

Perhaps the chief value of a Settlement to its neighborhood, certainly to the newly arrived foreigner, is its office as an information and interpretation bureau.

Jane Addams and her Hull House partner, Ellen G. Starr, drew support from businesspeople and others. Donations and income from her writings kept Hull House on a solid financial footing.

Addams also became active in the worldwide movements for peace and served as president of the Women's International League for Peace and Freedom. In 1931, she became the first American woman to be awarded the Nobel Peace Prize.

The Triangle Shirtwaist Fire

In 1911, a tragic fire in New York City at the Triangle Shirtwaist Company caused 146 deaths because the workers, mostly young women, could not get out of the upper floors. Exit doors had been locked so that workers wouldn't sneak out early, fire escapes collapsed, and the stairways were too narrow. The tragedy of the Triangle Shirtwaist factory fire contributed to a series of industrial safety laws in New York State. In the following reading, the social worker Frances Perkins describes the scene of the fire.

FROM

Frances Perkins's Account of the Triangle Shirtwaist Factory Fire

1 9 1 1

We saw the smoke pouring out of the building. We got there just as they started to jump. . . . They came down in twos and threes, jumping together in a kind of desperate hope.

The life nets were broken. The firefighters kept shouting for them not to jump. But they had no choice; the flames were right behind them. . . .

Out of that terrible episode came a self-examination . . . in which the people of this state saw for the first time the individual worth and value of each of those 146 people who fell or were burned. . . . There was a stricken conscience of public guilt and we all felt that we had been wrong, that something was wrong with that building which we had accepted or the tragedy never would have happened. . . . Out of the ashes of the tragedy rose the Factory Investigating Commission. It led the state legislature to pass tough protective laws.

Frances Perkins was one of the leaders of the progressive movement, working for improved conditions for workers. In 1933 President Franklin D. Roosevelt made her secretary of labor, the first woman named to a Cabinet position.

Theodore Roosevelt: A Progressive in the White House

On September 6, 1901, President William McKinley was shot by a lone gunman—Leon Czolgosz—in Buffalo, New York. McKinley died a few days later, and Vice President Theodore Roosevelt became the nation's president at the age of forty-two.

Roosevelt brought youthful energy and exuberance to the presidency. News reporters loved him because he was constantly in action, creating new headlines practically every day. The American people loved him because they felt he was on their side—a champion who would protect them from the overbearing power of big business.

The Assassination of President McKinley

President McKinley was at Buffalo's Pan-American Exposition when Leon Czolgocz, in the receiving line, shot the president at point-blank range. Czolgosz was an anarchist, a small political group that advocated anarchy—a society without government. To achieve this, they tried to get rid of government leaders by assassination. Although most active in Europe, there were a few anarchists in the United States, and they were often blamed for introducing violence into industrial strikes.

The first of the following readings is a reporter's account of how Roosevelt came to be president. The second selection is the journalist Mark Sullivan's assessment of what Teddy Roosevelt meant to the United States of the early 1900s. Sullivan was a news reporter who covered the presidency and national affairs from 1900 to 1925.

FROM

"T. R.'s Road to the White House"

1 9 0 2

In March 1901, Teddy Roosevelt took office as vice president, Congress adjourned and he had nothing to do, so he took a vacation to the Adirondacks. He was in some remote mountain camp when word came that President McKinley was dying from an assassin's bullet. Suddenly he found himself bouncing down a mountainside in a farm wagon, racing on the last leg of his journey to the presidency. How did it happen so fast? . . .

We all know that he was born into a wealthy New York family, and, weak and sickly as a boy, worked himself into a strong and vigorous athlete. He was *also* a scholar. His history of the *Naval War of 1812* is considered outstanding history. He is *also* something of an expert in several areas of natural science. He has *also* been a rancher in Dakota Territory at a time when the Indian Wars had not yet ended.

Above all else, Roosevelt has been a politician. Consider the record. He was a three-term assemblyman in New York. Then, losing a bid to become mayor, he used the influence of friends to be appointed to the Civil Service Commission in Washington and, four years later, became a member of the New York City police commission. There were three other men on that commission but the reporters loved Teddy and he was the only one they wrote about. Next, he was appointed Assistant Secretary of the Navy, attracting far more attention than the secretary.

The War with Spain sped Roosevelt even faster on his road to the White House, somehow emerging as the only national hero—except of course, for Commodore Dewey. What could the Republican bosses do with him? He was more popular than McKinley, and easily became governor of New York in 1898. So they made him McKinley's Vice President [in 1900]. What could be better, since even Teddy couldn't do much with that job—except to be ready when the message came that William McKinley was dying. . . . And now he's the youngest President in history.

FROM

Mark Sullivan's Our Times

1926

It is simple history to say that the relation Roosevelt had to America at this time, the power he was able to wield, the prestige he enjoyed, the affection he received, the contentment of the people with him— their more than contentment, their zesty pleasure in him—composed the lot of an exceptionally fortunate monarch during a particularly happy period of his reign. The basis of it was the fights Roosevelt made against organized wealth—the sum of which was that he had, in the plain sight of the common man, presented spectacle after spectacle in which business, capital, corporate power took off its hat in the presence of the symbol and spokesman of government. . . .

"Teddy" Roosevelt.

COURTESY, LIBRARY OF CONGRESS

What brought to Roosevelt the affection that few kings have had, and gave gay delight to the people was . . . certain qualities of his [personality], including "the fun of him." As one of his New York police captains remarked after his death—"It was not only that he was a great man, but, oh, there was such fun in being led by him." Roosevelt in battle, which was Roosevelt most of the time, was a huge personality endowed with energy almost abnormal, directed by an acute intelligence, lightened by a grinning humor, engaged in incessant action. The spectacle, occupying the biggest headlines in the daily newspapers, gave to the life of that day a zest and stimulus and gaiety such that average Americans who lived through the period carried it as a golden memory, sighing "there'll never be another Roosevelt," and telling their grandchildren that once they saw a giant.

Regulating Big Business

In the spring of 1902, President Roosevelt stunned the business world and thrilled the American public when he ordered his attorney general to start a lawsuit against a huge corporation called the Northern Securities Company. Northern Securities was a holding company (a company that has stock in several other companies in order to control them)—a sprawling railroad empire that had a monopoly on rail service in large areas of the nation. The head of the company was J. P. Morgan, the country's most powerful banker.

Morgan's lawyers fought the lawsuit that charged that the company was a monopoly—a company that has no competitors. In 1904, the Supreme Court ruled in favor of the government, and the holding company was divided into separate corporations.

In the following reading, Roosevelt explains why he thought the government had to interfere in business matters—a philosophy that continues to guide the U.S. government today.

FROM
Theodore Roosevelt's
The New Nationalism
1910

There is no effective state or national control upon unfair money-getting. This has tended to create a small class of enormously wealthy and powerful men, whose chief aim is to hold and increase their power. We need to change the conditions which allow these men to increase their power. We grudge no man a fortune which represents his own power and wisdom when exercised with regard to the welfare of his fellows. We should permit power to be gained only so long as the gaining represents benefit to the community. This, I know, requires far more governmental interference than we have yet had; I think we have got to face the fact that such an increase in governmental control is now necessary.

We are all Americans. Our common interests are as broad as the continent. The national government belongs to the whole American people. Where the whole American people are interested, that interest can be well guarded only by the national government. The improvement which we seek must be brought about, I believe, mainly by the national government.

One of the cartoons that made the "Teddy Bear" a permanent part of American culture.

COURTESY, LIBRARY OF CONGRESS

The Teddy Bear

In 1902, a cartoonist had fun with the president's refusal to shoot a bear cub during a hunting trip. According to legend, the incident inspired a Connecticut couple to produce a stuffed toy bear they called "the Teddy Bear," which became a big hit.

Roosevelt as Trustbuster

Theodore Roosevelt's goal was to fight bigness in business when that bigness was harmful to the people. For this reason he went after trusts—business organizations in which the stockholders of several corporations give control to a single board of trustees, or managers. Roosevelt always tried to distinguish between "good" trusts and "bad" trusts. He insisted that bigness was not wrong, as long as the public was not harmed. The government's role was to regulate big business, not to destroy it. During Roosevelt's presidency, a total of forty-four trusts were forced to break into smaller corporations.

Roosevelt's successors in the presidency—Republican William Howard Taft (1908–1912) and Democrat Woodrow Wilson (1912–1920)—actually broke up more trusts, but the public always associated this forceful method of regulation with Roosevelt.

Government Action for Public Health

In 1906, a novel by Upton Sinclair called *The Jungle* caused a sensation for its detailed description of unsanitary conditions in Chicago's meat-packing industry. President Roosevelt was skeptical, but he ordered an investigation, which revealed that conditions were even worse than Sinclair described.

At Roosevelt's urging, Congress passed the Meat Inspection Act in June 1906, providing for federal inspection of the industry. Congress also passed the Pure Food and Drug Act, banning the manufacture, transportation, or sale of impure foods and drugs. Misleading advertising was also outlawed. The next reading is one of the passages from *The Jungle* that helped start these first government actions to protect the American people from unhealthy foods and medicines.

The End of Progressivism

Progressive reforms continued after Roosevelt left office in 1909. (He had stated that he would not run for reelection in 1908.) Presidents William Howard Taft (1908–1912) and Woodrow Wilson (1912–1920) attacked trusts, tried to end child labor, and worked to improve conditions for workers and farmers. The years of progressive reforms ended in 1917 when the United States entered World War I.

FROM

Upton Sinclair's The Jungle

1906

There would be meat that had tumbled out on the floor, in the dirt and sawdust, where the workers had tramped and spit uncounted billions of **consumption** germs. There would be meat stored in great piles in rooms; and the water from leaky roofs would drip over it, and thousands of rats would race about on it.

It was too dark in these storage places to see well, but a man could run his hand over these piles of meat and sweep off handfuls of the dried dung of rats. These rats were nuisances, and the packers would put poisoned bread out for them; they would die, and then rats, bread, and meat would go into the hoppers together. This is no fairy story and no joke; the meat would be shoveled into carts, and the man who did the shoveling would not trouble to lift out a rat even when he saw one—there were things that went into the sausage in comparison with which a poisoned rat was a tidbit.

There was no place for the men to wash their hands before they ate their dinner, and so they made a practice of washing them in the water that was to be ladled into the sausage. There were the butt ends of smoked meat, and the scraps of corned beef, and all the odds and ends of the waste of the plants that would be dumped into old barrels in the cellar and left there.

Under the system of rigid economy which the packers enforced, there were some jobs that it only paid to do once in a long time, and among these was the cleaning out of the waste barrels. Every spring they did it; and in the barrels would be dirt and rust and old nails and stale water—and cartload after cartload of it would be taken up and dumped into the hoppers with fresh meat and sent out to the public's breakfast.

Chemists in the Roosevelt administration found that the average American meal included at least forty chemicals that the public was unaware of.

consumption: an outdated word for tuberculosis.

Uneven Progress for African Americans

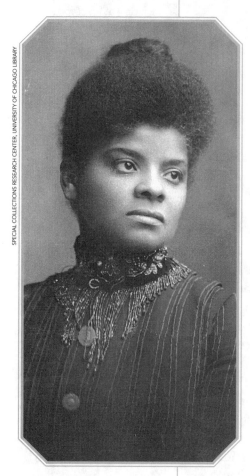

SPECIAL COLLECTIONS RESEARCH CENTER, UNIVERSITY OF CHICAGO LIBRARY

Ida B. Wells, the antilynching crusader.

Achieving racial equality was not a major part of the progressive agenda, but many African Americans continued to struggle for their rights. They wanted an end to the nation's increasingly strict segregation laws, especially in the South. An 1896 Supreme Court case, *Plessy v. Ferguson,* upheld those "Jim Crow" laws—laws that established separate facilities for blacks, ranging from theater seats to drinking fountains. The Court ruled that separate facilities for blacks were perfectly legal (although they were supposed to be equal to white facilities).

The following reading is from an article by Ida B. Wells, part of her one-woman crusade to end the lynching of African Americans. She fought this crusade throughout her career as a journalist. Her research showed that, between 1878 and 1898, more than nine thousand African Americans had been lynched. Lynching—executing someone, usually by hanging, without a trial—had become a major weapon of racist white groups. Many believed that creating the fear of being lynched was a way to prevent blacks from trying to exercise basic rights, like the right to vote. Wells's exposure of this kind of violence against blacks led a group of whites and blacks to form the National Association for the Advancement of Colored People (NAACP) in 1909. Working primarily through the courts, the NAACP continues to champion the rights of African Americans in the twenty-first century.

FROM

"Original Rights," by Ida B. Wells

1910

The record of the past ten years shows a surprising increase in lynchings and riot even in the North. No northern state has more frequently offended in this crime than Illinois, the state of Lincoln. . . . Since 1893 there have been sixteen lynchings within the state, including the Springfield riot. With each repetition there has been increased violence, rioting, and barbarism. The last lynching, which took place November 11 of last year in Cairo, was one of the most inhuman spectacles ever witnessed in this country. A white girl had been found murdered two days before. The bloodhounds which were brought led to a Negro's house three blocks away. A Negro who had stayed in that house the night before was arrested. . . . Threats of lynching him became so frequent that the sheriff took him away from the city, back in the woods twenty-five miles away.

When the mob had increased its numbers, they chartered a train, went after the sheriff, [and] brought him and his prisoner back to Cairo. A rope was thrown over [the prisoner] Will James's neck; he was dragged off the train to the main business corner of the town. The rope was thrown over a steel arch, which had a double row of electric lights. The lights were turned on and the body hauled up in view of the assembled thousands of men, women and children.

Women's Right to Vote

In 1915, a huge parade for women's voting rights took place in New York City. By this time, thousands of women felt no shame in marching in a "suffragist" parade; more and more men supported the cause, and President Wilson stated that women's suffrage was vital to the war effort. In January 1918, the House finally passed the Nineteenth Amendment, giving women the right to vote. More than two more years were needed, however, to complete the process of ratification. The following reading is a young middle-class woman's account of taking part in the parade.

FROM

Outlook *Magazine*

JUNE 1915

I didn't walk in New York's first suffrage parade because my mother wouldn't let me. Next year, in 1913, I wanted to march, but my husband asked me not to. This fall I decided that it was "up to me" to suffer for democracy.

Three o'clock on the afternoon of October 23, and a glorious day. Every band in Greater New York and some beyond blows like the breeze today. . . .

By the time we had gone two blocks I had forgotten everything I had expected to feel. All my girlhood Mother had repeated that a lady should never allow herself to be conspicuous. To march up Fifth Avenue had promised to flout directly one's early training. I was mistaken. There's no notoriety about it. When it's done along with twenty-five thousand other women, nothing could seem more natural. Embarrassment is left at the street corner, and one is just a part, a singing, swinging part of a great stream, all flowing in the same direction toward the same goal. . . .

They tell us that two hundred and fifty thousand people watched us walk from Washington Square to Sixtieth Street. From sunlight till the moon came out, the chilly sidewalks never once were clear of the curious.

Suffragettes in action. By 1916, as many as 10,000 marched in parades in Washington, D.C.

PART III

AMERICA IN THE FIRST WORLD WAR

In June 1914, an Austro-Hungarian archduke and his wife were assassinated in the central European city of Sarajevo. That tragedy brought to a head the conflicts that had been brewing in Europe and touched off a chain of events that plunged the continent and much of the world into the most devastating war in history up to that time. This was the first war in which modern weapons were used: airplanes, submarines, and tanks. No one was prepared for the destructive force of these weapons, and people were repeatedly shocked by the reports of the numbers of killed and wounded.

For the first two years of the conflict, Americans spoke of the "European War"; it seemed to have little to do with life in the United States. By the time of the Armistice (truce) in 1918, people were referring to it as the "Great War." A few years later, when war again erupted and it became clear that this had not been the "war to end all wars," it became known as World War I.

The readings in this part deal with how the United States became involved in the war, how the conflict affected Americans, and why the outcome led the nation to try to isolate itself from Europe.

World War I: From Neutrality to War

When the war began in August 1914, President Woodrow Wilson was determined to steer a neutral course, even as the conflict engulfed nearly all of Europe and many other countries. Germany and its allies, known as the Central Powers, struck quickly, driving through Belgium and deep into France. But France and its major ally, Great Britain, known with other countries as the Allied Powers, stopped the advance just short of Paris. For the next three years, the war on the western front settled into grim trench warfare, with Germans and Allied troops facing each other across a front of opposing trenches that stretched nearly 600 miles.

Quite early in the conflict, it became clear that most Americans sympathized with the Allied powers. Britain and France were fellow democracies, while Germany was a militaristic nation ruled by a king, called a kaiser.

People were also horrified by the way Germany used their submarines. In 1915, a German U-boat, or submarine, torpedoed and sank the British liner *Lusitania,* with 128 Americans among the nearly 1,200 killed. In the past, warships followed international tradition by warning ships carrying passengers before attacking and, when a ship was sunk, picking up survivors. But submarines attacked without notice and their commanders had no way of rescuing any survivors. Formal U.S. protests led Germany to suspend submarine warfare for nearly two years. When Germany announced the renewal of "unrestricted submarine warfare" early in 1917, it pushed the United States a giant step closer to declaring war.

A few weeks after that announcement, British agents intercepted and decoded a secret telegram from a German official to Mexico. This "Zimmermann Note," made public by the Wilson administration, was a German promise that, in exchange for an alliance, Germany would help Mexico regain its "lost territory"— Texas, New Mexico, Arizona, and California. The outraged American people fully supported President Wilson's response, asking Congress for a declaration of war against Germany.

Allied Powers

Belgium	Italy
Brazil	Japan
British Empire	Liberia
China	Panama
Costa Rica	Portugal
Cuba	Romania
France	Russia
Greece	Serbia
Guatemala	Siam
Haiti	United States
Honduras	

Central Powers

Austro-Hungarian Empire
Bulgaria
German Empire
Ottoman Empire (Turkey)

The following readings present an excerpt from the Zimmermann Note, statements from Wilson's war message, and a letter from a young woman to her army boyfriend stationed in France, informing him that she has become a "leatherneck," or marine.

FROM

The "Zimmermann Note"

MARCH 1917

[We] intend to begin submarine warfare unrestricted. In spite of this, it is our intention to [try] to keep neutral the United States. . . .

If this attempt is not successful, we propose an alliance on the following basis with Mexico: That we shall make war together and together make peace. We shall give general financial support, and it is understood that Mexico is to recover the lost territory in New Mexico, California, Texas, and Arizona. The details are left to you for settlement.

FROM

President Wilson's War Message to Congress

APRIL 2, 1917

Neutrality is no longer feasible or desirable when the peace of the world is involved and the freedom of its peoples. . . . We have no quarrel with the German people. We have no feeling towards them but one of sympathy and friendship. . . .

The world must be made safe for democracy. . . . We have no selfish ends to serve. We desire no conquest, no dominion. We seek no . . . material compensation for the sacrifices we shall freely make. We are but one of the champions of the rights of mankind. We shall be satisfied when these rights have been made as secure as the faith and the freedom of nations can make them.

With a profound sense of the solemn and even tragical character of the step I am taking and of the grave responsibilities which it involves, but in unhesitating obedience to what I deem my constitutional duty, I advise that the Congress declare the recent course of the Imperial German government to be, in fact, nothing less than war against the government and people of the United States.

The War on the Home Front

The American people went to war in 1917 with tremendous patriotic spirit. American "doughboys" (popular slang for the U.S. infantrymen) marched past cheering crowds, with bands playing, and every main street decked out in red-white-and-blue bunting. People were certain that, as President Wilson said, they were going to Europe to "make the world safe for democracy."

The entire population was involved in the war effort as never before in history. Farms and industries turned out ever-increasing amounts of foodstuffs and war materials, not only for the millions of men in the military, but for the Allies in war-torn Europe. People were willing to accept far more government interference in their lives. The government Railroad Administration, for example, took over the management of the country's railroads in order to control the movement of troops and supplies, and the Fuel Administration decided how much fuel Americans could use in their homes and businesses.

New York's famous "Rainbow Division," with soldiers from twenty-six states, marches past cheering crowds, 1917.

GEORGE EASTMAN HOUSE

FROM

"The First Lady Marine"

1917

Dear Bill,

I've got the greatest news! No, I haven't thrown you over! I'm still strong for you, Bill. . . . Are you ready? Well then, I'm a lady leatherneck. . . . I'm a real, live honest-to-goodness Marine! . . .

When I heard they had at last hung out a sign at the recruiting station—"Women wanted for the United States Marine Corps"—I was ready. "Mother," says I, "give me your blessing; I'm going to be the first to enlist." I was there when the doors opened in the morning. I was one of the first all right—the first 600! You'd think they were selling sugar or something. Well, when the crowd heard that you had to be willing to go anywhere as ordered and you had to be a cracker-jack stenographer, they thinned out some. . . . Well, only three of us came out alive. . . .

Bill, I soon learned I wasn't going to shoot any Huns [Germans]. In fact, just about all us Marinettes will end up working as typists or stenogs on this side of the Atlantic. . . . But we wear a uniform and wear it with pride. We know that each of us makes it possible for a male Marine with an itchy trigger finger to go over there and start shooting.

A U.S. Marine recruiting poster. For the first time in history, women wore military uniforms and thousands served in non-combat roles.

World War I was the first time women were ever recruited for U.S. military service. They were not sent into combat, but they did wear uniforms and sometimes had dangerous assignments. Only 269 women served in the marines, about 50,000 in the army, and about 11,000 in the navy. They were far more numerous in taking on industry and other jobs left vacant by men who went into the military. Women drove ambulances, worked on assembly lines, delivered mail, and worked in offices. Thousands of women became nurses and many worked in hospitals in France and England.

IF YOU WANT TO FIGHT! JOIN THE MARINES

COURTESY, LIBRARY OF CONGRESS

The Government and Public Opinion

President Wilson wanted to be certain that the American people were solidly behind the war effort. He established a Committee on Public Information headed by a journalist named George Creel. Creel proceeded to use every device of persuasion—or propaganda—to "sell" the war as a great crusade of good against evil. He hired writers, painters, lecturers, actors, and others to flood the nation with posters, pamphlets, speeches, and movies. The Creel Committee helped to create a fever of anti-German feeling.

Another dimension of the government's campaign for public opinion was the determination to silence anyone who opposed or even criticized the war effort. The Espionage Act of June 1917 provided penalties for anyone who helped the enemy or encouraged disobedience. In May 1918, the Sedition Act made it a crime to say or write anything disloyal about the government, the United States, the Constitution, the flag, or U.S. military uniforms. The following reading was a reaction to this "patriotism at all costs."

Prohibition

Laws prohibiting the manufacture, sale, or transportation of alcoholic beverages had already gone into effect in most states of the West and South. Then, in 1917, many progressives saw it as part of the nation's war effort. They reasoned that the grain used to make alcohol would be better used to make bread for America's troops and the Allies. Many also thought that the ban would reduce absenteeism in factories and shops. In December 1918, Congress approved the Eighteenth Amendment and it went into effect the following year, making it a federal offense to manufacture, sell, or transport alcoholic beverages. The Volstead Act, passed in January 1919, provided for enforcement.

FROM

The Buffalo Courier

JULY 1918

At some time soon, and Independence Day would be a place to start, the current "patriotism" at all costs will be replaced by our freedom of speech and even freedom to hold dissenting opinions. The loyal German-Americans in our city and nation have been accused of being traitors simply because they, or their parents, were born in Germany. We see signs insisting that sauerkraut is now "liberty cabbage" and hamburger is "liberty sausage." We may laugh at these outrages, but we cannot laugh when Boston fires its distinguished symphony conductor because he is of German birth, or that other symphonies refuse to play the works of Beethoven and others. And perhaps the most dangerous insult was the recent burning of books by German authors in Wisconsin. . . . Wisconsin, like Buffalo, has loyal German-American citizens, some of whom have sent their sons to fight the Kaiser's armies.

American Forces in Europe

By the time the United States entered the war in April 1917, Britain, France, and the other Allies were exhausted by nearly three years of warfare. The Germans were also war-weary, but two events in 1917 gave them a new advantage. First, in southern Europe, the Italian armies were crushed by German and Austrian troops, forcing the Allies to send reinforcements. Then, in Russia, the Russian Bolsheviks—a wing of the Communist party—overthrew the government and began peace talks with Germany. This allowed the German High Command to move thousands of troops from the Russian front to France.

The entrance of the United States into the war, therefore, came at a crucial time, especially when it became clear that the Germans were planning one decisive assault for 1918. The question was whether the United States could train a large enough army and transport it to France in time to help blunt the German attack. By June 1917, U.S. commander General John J. Pershing was in France with a few thousand men. He allowed some troops to fight with French units, for experience, but he insisted that the U.S. divisions fight separately from British and French armies.

The first of the following readings is from a telegram from General Pershing to Washington, D.C., on the bravery of African American troops. The second selection is from one of the most popular songs of the war. Written by George M. Cohan, it expresses a good deal of the doughboys' cocky, determined attitude as they headed overseas.

Some of the sentences in General Pershing's telegram are choppy because, in sending a telegram—or cable—the writer tries to use as few words as possible.

Crois de Guerre: The "War Cross" was the highest award France gave to foreigners. America's African American troops won 150 of these medals during the war.

FROM
General Pershing's Cable to Washington
JUNE 1918

To Adjutant General
Washington   Confidential

[The training of African American troops] is identical with that of other American troops serving with the French Army, the effort being to lead all American troops gradually to heavy combat duty by preliminary service in trenches in quiet sectors. Colored troops in trenches have been particularly fortunate, as one regiment had been there a month before any losses were suffered. This almost unheard of on western front.

Exploit of colored infantrymen some weeks ago repelling much larger German patrol killing and wounding several Germans and winning *Crois de Guerre* by their gallantry has roused fine spirit of emulation throughout colored troops all of whom are looking forward to more active service. Only regret expressed by colored troops is that they are not given more dangerous work to do. They are especially amused at the stories being circulated that the American colored troops are placed in the most dangerous positions and all are desirous of having more active service than has been permitted them thus far. I cannot commend too highly the spirit shown among the colored combat troops who exhibit fine capacity for quick training and eagerness for the most dangerous work.

Pershing

FROM

"Over There"

1917

Over there, over there,
Send the word, send the word over
  there,
That the Yanks are coming, the Yanks
  are coming,
The drums rum-tumming every-
  where.
So prepare, say a prayer,
Send the word, send the word to
  beware
We'll be over, we're coming over,
And we won't come back till it's
  over over there.

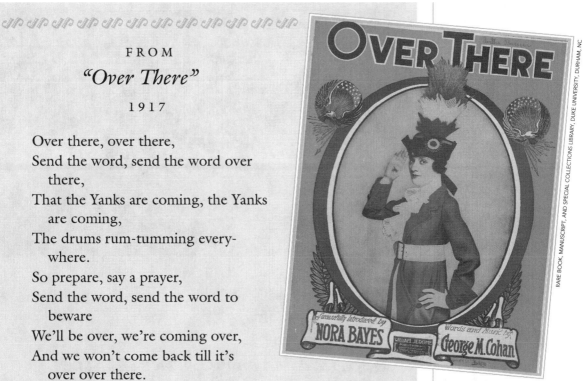

Sheet music for George M. Cohan's "Over There," one of the most popular songs of World War I.

Trench Warfare

When the first U.S. soldiers began arriving in France in June 1917, the opposing armies faced each other from trenches that stretched nearly 600 miles from the North Sea to the border of Switzerland. The trenches were usually about 2 feet wide and 5 feet deep, with rolls of barbed wire in front. Beyond was "No Man's Land"—open ground that had to be crossed to reach the enemy's trenches.

An attack was signaled by hours of artillery fire. Then the infantry would go "over the top," charging across No Man's Land, often supported by tanks, hoping to find a hole in the enemy's line. If the battle was a success, the attacking force might gain a few hundred yards of territory, but at a terrible cost in killed, wounded, and missing. In the following two readings, two doughboys describe this grim aspect of the war.

American "doughboys" learned to use war's deadly new weapons, such as machine guns.

COURTESY OF U.S. NATIONAL ARCHIVES AT COLLEGE PARK, MD

FROM

An Anonymous Soldier's Account

1917

[We] come along, and in military parlance "dig ourselves in." That is, with the sweat of the brows of hundreds of [soldiers] working by night narrow trenches [are dug] five feet deep at least and with the earth thrown up another two and a half feet as a bank on top. These trenches are one and a half to two feet wide, and curl and twist about in a maddening manner to make them safer from shellfire. Little caves are scooped in the walls of the trenches, where the men live about four to a hole, and slightly bigger dugouts where two officers live. All the soil is clay, stickier and greasier than one could believe possible. It's like almost solid paint, and the least rain makes the sides of the trenches slimy, and the bottom a perfect sea of mud—pulls the heels off your boots almost. . . . The front line of trenches—the firing-line—have . . . loopholes and look-out places in them for seeing and firing from, and a dropping fire goes on from both sides all day long.

FROM

The Diary of Norman Roberts

1918

Sept. 12. At 5:00 A.M. the words came down the trench to get ready for attack. Over the top we are going after **Fritz**. I was the fourth man of my platoon to go over. . . . Day had not broke and you could hardly tell where to go. Bullets, millions of them, flying like raindrops. Rockets and flares in all directions. Shrapnel bursting the air and sending down its deadly iron. High explosives bursting in the ground and sending forth bricks, mud, and iron to the destruction of man. Oh, what a morning. Machine gun bullets flying past you as the wind.

Dead and wounded all around you. Comrades falling directly in front and you not allowed to assist them. The command *onward*. Every minute looking for the next to be gone to the great beyond. A mad dash for fifty feet and then look for cover. A stop for a minute and then the barrage would lift to a farther point and then another mad rush. Always leaving some of your comrades cold in the face of death. Men crying for the Almighty God to have mercy upon them. Asking the men to shoot them and place them out of their misery. . . .

Airplanes sweeping down upon you and firing their guns almost in your face. Barbed wire in all directions. I became tangled in this and thought surely before I could free myself that I would be killed. We have supremacy of the air during this battle. Day breaks and oh, how pleased to welcome same.

Fritz: slang for German soldiers.

Battle of Verdun

One of the bloodiest battles of the trench war was the Battle of Verdun, which began in February 1916 with a German assault on that French city. Day after day the two sides pounded at each other, sometimes one side trying an attack, then the other. After 6 months, an estimated 40,000,000 artillery shells had churned the land into a moonscape of mud, shell craters, and shattered trees. The Germans advanced their line about 4 miles, but suffered 300,000 casualties (killed, wounded, and missing). The French held on to Verdun but at a cost of 350,000 casualties.

The Silent Weapon: Poison Gas

The Role of the U.S. Navy

The U.S. navy played a vital role in reducing the menace of German submarines. American and British ships placed about 70,000 mines in the North Sea, making it hard for the U-boats to reach the open sea from German ports. The two navies also developed a convoy system—having ships cross the Atlantic in groups, with warships providing protection. What was called the "Bridge of Ships" enabled the transporting of more than two million soldiers from the United States to France without losing a single ship.

One of the deadly new weapons created by twentieth-century science was poison gas—silent, killing clouds that could descend over enemy positions, choking or blinding the men who were not equipped with gas masks, or didn't get them on quickly enough. The two kinds of gas used in World War I—chlorine gas and mustard gas—killed thousands and left thousands more blind or with damaged lungs. In the reading that follows, a lieutenant tries to reassure his wife that he is not in serious danger.

FROM

Lieutenant Ed Lukert's Letter to His Wife

JUNE 1918

Do you smell gas also? We were all subjected to several different kinds of it today, with and without masks, and as usual, I cannot rid my clothes of the odor. It is sure awful stuff, honey. Deadly and usually insures a slow horrible death. There is one kind which kills quickly, Chlorine, but I do not prefer any kind or brand myself. I'll use the gas mask if possible, with all its discomforts and smell. . . .

There's no danger tho. You'll have me back soon. The war cannot last forever, you know, and even if it does, I will return to you safe and sound eventually.

The War in the Air

The Wright brothers had made the first airplane flight only eleven years before the start of the war, and it was 1908 before either the public or the military showed any interest. The war led to rapid advances in airplane technology, and wartime pilots soon learned to equip their fragile craft with machine guns, introducing a dramatic and entertaining aspect to the war. Even soldiers on the ground enjoyed watching the aerial "dogfights" in the skies over France, and they came to know the planes of the "aces" on both sides.

Many Americans were eager to join the daring and dashing aviators, and the few Yank fliers caught on quickly, using French or British planes. The first-ever American air combat group was not formed until April 1918, but over the remaining 7 months of the war, 44 more squadrons were formed, with a total of 650 aviators. These newcomers shot down 781 German aircraft, with Eddie Rickenbacker's 26 "kills" making him the first American ace.

Although the air war was colorful and romantic, it had little impact on the course of the war. The reading in this section is from a letter written by Quentin Roosevelt, the youngest son of former president Theodore Roosevelt.

Eddie Rickenbacker, America's air ace, credited with downing twenty-six German planes.

FROM

Quentin Roosevelt's Letter Home

JULY 1918

I was out on patrol with the rest of my squadron when we got broken up due to a mistake in formation. . . . I turned and circled for five minutes or so, then suddenly . . . I saw three planes in formation. . . . Thinking they were part of my crowd, I started after them at full speed . . . and I was nearly in formation when the leader did a turn and I saw to my horror that they had white tails with black crosses on them. Still I was so near to them that I thought I might pull up a little and take a crack at them. I had altitude on them, and . . . they hadn't seen me . . . so I put my sights on the end man and let go. I saw my **tracers** going all around him, but for some reason he never turned, until all of a sudden his tail came up and he went down in a **vrille.** I wanted to follow him but the other two had started around after me, so I had to cut and run. However, I could half watch him by looking back, and he was still spinning when he hit the clouds four thousand feet below.

tracers: machine gun bullets that left a red trail.

vrille: French for "dive."

The Road to Victory

In mid-July the Germans tried one more furious lunge at Paris and they were confident the British and French were about to surrender. But 270,000 Yanks helped turn back the German advance, and General Ludendorff, the head of the German army, said, "On the 18th [of July] even the most optimistic among us knew that all was lost."

In September 1918 the Allies launched a massive counteroffensive along the entire front. A U.S. force of 550,000 captured St. Mihiel, a vital railroad junction, and then more than one million doughboys advanced through the Argonne Forest in one of the most vicious battles of the war. For forty-seven days, they inched their way through the forest and, in spite of heavy losses, reached Sedan on November 7, cutting the Germans' railroad supply line. On November 11, 1918, Germany signed the Armistice ending the war.

The next selection is a description of a few hours in the Argonne Forest by a communications specialist, twenty-one-year-old Elmer Sherwood.

The Human Cost of the War

The major armies involved in the war lost more than half of their troops—killed, wounded, or missing in action. A total of nearly nine million were killed. Germany and France had the greatest losses—roughly one out of every thirty people died of war-related causes in both countries.

The psychological costs of the war were also severe. Simply witnessing the mass destruction was a traumatic shock to many. In addition, in Germany, some men were determined to avenge their nation's defeat, including a wounded corporal named Adolf Hitler.

FROM

Corporal Elmer Sherwood's Diary

OCTOBER 30, 1918

Last night Fritz put on a whale of a bombardment, and I don't see how any of us escaped to tell the story. In the thick of it our communications were knocked out and I was detailed to repair the telephone line. How kind they are to me! Well, I breathed a little prayer, climbed out of my fox-hole, and darted out into the inferno.

Flashes of exploding artillery at intervals lighted up the blackness of the night. Explosions of enemy shells on every hand and the scream of big ones going overhead to back areas added to the thunderous uproar so that I could not have heard my own voice had I dared to speak. Boy! I was glad when I came to the break in the line. I was splicing the wire when—Shriek! Bang! A ton of steel came over me. Just as I finished the job . . . another hit knocked the line out in another place.

For once I lost my cocky self-assurance, and I wasn't so certain I would ever see home and Mother again. But finally, after stumbling over the body of a dead German, I came upon the next break and spliced it in a hurry. Then I raced back to my hole after reporting communications in order. Jack has just been sent back to the hospital with **shell-shock,** No wonder nerves give way and normal men go crazy.

shell-shock: uncontrollable shaking as a nervous reaction to the noise and danger.

President Wilson's Fourteen Points

In January 1918 President Woodrow Wilson had announced his plan for creating a more peaceful world after the war. This plan, called the Fourteen Points, called on the nations to agree on certain principles, including:

- Open agreements between countries, rather than secret treaties

- Freedom of navigation on the sea in peace and war

- Free trade between countries

- An association of nations to guarantee the peace

Part of Wilson's speech explaining the points follows.

COURTESY, LIBRARY OF CONGRESS

President Woodrow Wilson

FROM

President Woodrow Wilson's Fourteen Points

1918

It will be our wish and purpose that the processes of peace, when they are begun, shall be absolutely open and that they shall involve and permit henceforth no secret understandings of any kind. The day of conquest and aggrandizement is gone by; so is also the day of secret covenants entered into in the interest of particular governments and likely at some unlooked-for moment to upset the peace of the world. It is this happy fact, now clear to the view of every public man whose thoughts do not still linger in an age that is dead and gone, which makes it possible for every nation whose purposes are consistent with justice and the peace of the world to avow nor or at any other time the objects it has in view.

We entered this war because violations of right had occurred which touched us to the quick and made the life of our own people impossible unless they were corrected and the world secure once for all against their recurrence. What we demand in this war, therefore, is nothing peculiar to ourselves. It is that the world be made fit and safe to live in; and particularly that it be made safe for every peace-loving nation which, like our own, wishes to live its own life, determine its own institutions, be assured of justice and fair dealing by the other peoples of the world as against force and selfish aggression. All the peoples of the world are in effect partners in this interest, and for our own part we see very clearly that unless justice be done to others it will not be done to us.

People throughout the world hailed the Fourteen Points. It seemed to be a plan that could make something positive out of this nightmarish war. When Wilson arrived in France, however, after the war for peace treaty talks at Versailles, outside Paris, he was stunned to find that France and Britain were no longer interested in his Fourteen Points. Instead, the Allied leaders wanted to punish the Germans for the war and make sure that they did not start another. The resulting peace treaty was harsh. Germany had to accept full responsibility for starting the war and had to agree to pay billions of dollars in damages. These vengeful conditions left the German people bitter, and the new German government, the country's first democracy, had to take the blame for signing the treaty. The commander of the Allied armies, French marshal Ferdinand Foch, said, "This is not a peace. It is an armistice for twenty years." Foch was right. World War II began exactly twenty years later.

Wilson did not return to the United States completely empty-handed, and he still had great hope in the League of Nations. The American people, however, had been disillusioned by the war; they wanted to turn their backs on Europe and get back to peacetime pursuits. In the Senate, a group of powerful Republicans were intent on rejecting the treaty, particularly the League of Nations. The leader of the Republicans, Senator Henry Cabot Lodge of Massachusetts, actually hoped to get the Senate to ratify (approve) the treaty, but he insisted on so many changes that Wilson refused to compromise. Convinced that the American people would support him, the president launched a nationwide speaking tour, visiting twenty-nine cities in twenty-two days, but already worn out, Wilson collapsed and was rushed back to Washington where he suffered a stroke that left him partially paralyzed. On May 20, 1920, the treaty was defeated in the Senate.

The United States then entered a twenty-year period of isolationism—trying to isolate itself from the world's troubles. And the League of Nations struggled to maintain peace without U.S. participation. The following selection presents part of Lodge's argument against the league.

꧁ ꧁ ꧁ ꧁ ꧁ ꧁ ꧁ ꧁ ꧁ ꧁ ꧁ ꧁ ꧁ ꧁ ꧁

FROM

A Speech by Henry Cabot Lodge

1919

I object in the strongest possible way to having the United States agree, directly or indirectly, to be controlled by a league which may at any time, and perfectly lawfully and in accordance with the terms of the Covenant, be drawn in to deal with internal conflicts in other countries, no matter what those conflicts may be. We should never permit the United States to be involved in any internal conflict in another country, except by the will of her people expressed through the Congress which represents them. . . .

We may set aside all this empty talk about isolation. Nobody expects to isolate the United States or make it a hermit nation, which is sheer absurdity. But there is a wide difference between taking a suitable part and bearing a due responsibility in world affairs and plunging the United States into every controversy and conflict on the face of the globe. . . .

The United States is the world's best hope, but if you fetter her in the interests and quarrels of other nations, if you tangle her in the intrigues of Europe, you will destroy her power for good and endanger her very existence.

President Wilson's Gains

Although President Wilson failed to have the United States sign the treaty or join the league, the League of Nations was organized. The very fact that so many of the world's nations were willing to take some responsibility for preventing war represented a great step forward for humankind.

Wilson's idea of self-determination also produced major changes in the map of central Europe. All the old empires had collapsed during the war, including the German, the Russian, and the Austro-Hungarian. Out of the remnants, a number of new nations were formed, providing independence for groups that had been oppressed minorities. The new nations included Finland, Estonia, Latvia, Lithuania, Poland, Czechoslovakia, Austria, Hungary, and Yugoslavia.

PART IV

The "Roaring Twenties"

The doughboys returned from the Great War to a nation still in transition. The Census of 1920 showed that, for the first time in the nation's history, more Americans lived in cities and large towns than in rural areas. Some rural people didn't like what was happening; they felt that the old ways and the old values were slipping away. One characteristic of the 1920s would be the sometimes desperate struggle of conservative Americans to stop this great wave of change.

Most Americans embraced the changes. They had more money and more leisure time than ever before, and there was more to spend it on. There were glittering new things to buy—automobiles, radios, cameras, washing machines, vacuum cleaners, and dozens of other appliances and gadgets. There were new forms of entertainment like automobile trips, motion pictures, jazz bands, and spectator sports. Alcoholic beverages were outlawed during the period of Prohibition, but that only provided the slight danger of drinking at illegal "speakeasies" and the fun of reading about gangsters like Al Capone. And for many this was a time for "flaming youth" to rebel against their parents and against custom.

The readings in this part provide glimpses of the decade people called the "Roaring Twenties."

America on Wheels

Perhaps no other invention has created such swift and sweeping changes as the automobile. The motor vehicle itself was developed slowly through the work of several inventors during the 1890s. By 1910, the few thousand automobiles in the United States were still toys for the wealthy. Each was crafted by hand, with beautiful accents in brass, copper, leather, and wood.

Henry Ford changed all that and almost single-handedly "put the nation on wheels." The key to lowering costs so that the average family could afford an automobile was Ford's development of assembly-line production. Every car was made up of identical parts and each worker did only a few tasks. Between 1909 and 1925, Ford made only one vehicle—the Model T—and sold fifteen million of them.

The assembly line was so successful that the price of a Ford Model T dropped steadily—from $900 in 1908 to $290 in 1926.

Henry Ford's Model T, 1915, one of more than 15 million "Tin Lizzies."

COURTESY, LIBRARY OF CONGRESS

The automobile boom led to massive road building throughout the country. Even where no paved roads yet existed, hearty motorists headed in all directions, following country lanes and courageously crossing farm fields.

The selections that follow provide information on Henry Ford's role in the development of the automobile and how motor vehicles transformed American life.

Ford and Labor

Ford was proud of the fact that the company hired many handicapped workers. More than four hundred of the men were amputees. Ford felt that work gave people dignity.

In 1914 Ford astounded the nation by reducing the workday from ten to eight hours and doubling each worker's daily wage to five dollars.

FROM

Henry Ford's My Life and Work

1 9 2 2

The undirected worker spends more of his time walking about for materials and tools than he does in working. . . .

The first step forward in assembly came when we began taking the work to the men instead of the men to the work. We now have two general principles in all operations— that a man shall never have to take more than one step, if possibly it can be avoided, and that no man need ever stoop over. . . .

Along about April 1, 1913, we tried the first experiment of an assembly line. . . . I believe that was the first moving line ever installed. The idea came in a general way from the overhead trolley that the Chicago packers use in dressing beef. . . .

We tried the experiment of drawing the chassis . . . down a line two hundred fifty feet long. Six assemblers traveled with the chassis and picked up parts from piles placed along the way. This rough experiment reduced the time from twelve hours and twenty-eight minutes to five hours fifty minutes per chassis. . . . We made improvements almost every day thereafter.

꧁ ꧁ ꧁ ꧁ ꧁ ꧁ ꧁ ꧁ ꧁ ꧁ ꧁ ꧁ ꧁ ꧁

FROM

"The Road to Freedom," Motor Car

1922

You are your master; the road is ahead; you eat as you please, cooking your own meals over an open fire; sleeping when you will under the stars, waking with the dawn; swim in a mountain lake when you will, and always the road ahead. The [wilderness] at 29 cents a gallon. . . . Time and space is at your beck and call; your freedom is complete.

The Automobile Boom

By the late 1920s, the automobile industry was the nation's largest, and it touched many other parts of the economy. The production of steel, rubber, gasoline, and glass increased dramatically. Workers were needed for assembly lines and for gasoline-and-repair stations. Over 100,000 miles of roads were being paved and every mile of highway sprouted "tourist homes," campgrounds, hotdog stands, and billboards.

The Deluxe Movie Theaters

The first motion pictures were developed in the 1890s and early 1900s by Thomas Edison and others. Viewers saw a minute-long silent film by peering through a peep-hole. These "nickelodeons" were popular for several years until replaced by scenes projected onto a screen. From the first full-length film in 1903—*The Great Train Robbery*—movies developed rapidly. By the early 1920s, every town had a movie theater and large cities each had several deluxe movie theaters, as described in the next reading.

Until 1927, the movies were silent. Dialogue was printed, and music was provided by a piano, an organ, or a small orchestra. In 1927, *The Jazz Singer,* starring Al Jolson, became the first "talkie."

FROM

Lloyd Lewis's "The Deluxe Picture Palace"

1929

The builders planned their new theater on an unprecedented scale, lined its interior with crimson velvet and marble, adorned the walls with paintings, and filled the lobbies with uniformed and bowing ushers. In a swirl of color and splendor, they experimented with prologues, singers, dancers in diaphanous robes, and "presentations"—in fact, almost everything that the most gorgeous of the 6,000-seat "de luxe" houses offer, on a still vaster scale, today.

By 1926, almost every large city had its "de luxe" house, seating from 2,500 to 4,500 people. Small picture houses died around them like flies. In cities of less than 200,000 inhabitants, the legitimate theaters wilted. . . .

But each year the "de luxe" houses were more thronged. That pioneer, the Central Park, played to 750,000 patrons in its first year. In 1928, the circuit of Chicago theaters, to which it still belongs, had expanded to include twelve, the other eleven all larger than their progenitor, and had checked over 30,000,000 admissions in the year.

When the theater patron goes home that evening, she will perhaps clean spinach and peel onions, but for a few hours, attendants bow to her, doormen tip their hats, and a maid curtsies to her in the ladies' washroom. She bathes in elegance and dignity; she satisfies her yearning for a "cultured" atmosphere. Even the hush that hangs over the lobbies means refinement to her: voices that have been raucous on the street drop, as they drop on entering a church.

Hollywood and Movie Stars

By 1920, the motion picture industry had made its home in Hollywood to take advantage of the sunshine and climate. Newspapers and magazines publicized the great stars, filling their pages with gossip and photographs, helping to create Hollywood's storied glitter and glamour. Mary Pickford, Douglas Fairbanks, and Rudolph Valentino were among the romantic stars, while Charlie Chaplin, Buster Keaton, and the Keystone Cops were the comedy leaders.

GETTY IMAGES

Silent movie heartthrob Rudolph Valentino.

The Heroic Age in Sports

Spectators and Participants

In the 1920s, Americans became spectators of sports in remarkable numbers. More than thirty million people attended big-league baseball games each year and there were dozens of minor leagues. When heavyweight boxers Jack Dempsey and Gene Tunney met in their second fight at Soldiers' Field in Chicago, a crowd of 120,000 was on hand and an estimated 50 million followed the radio account.

Americans were avid participants in sports as well. Eighty-nine cities built municipal golf courses during the 1920s. In 1903, only 18 cities had public playgrounds and parks; by 1924 that number had grown to more than 6,000 parks in 680 communities. In addition, almost every business sponsored amateur or semiprofessional teams that competed in baseball, golf, basketball, and track and field.

Leisure time, money, and the mass media combined to make the 1920s the "Golden Age of Sports." The heroes of the decade, and their exploits, all seemed larger than life. Baseball legend George Herman "Babe" Ruth was special, partly because he constantly punished his body with excessive eating and drinking, but was still *the* great power hitter of his day. When Ruth belted his record sixty home runs in 1927, all the other teams in the American League combined didn't hit that many.

Every sport produced its towering heroes: Jack Dempsey and Gene Tunney in boxing; Red Grange and Knute Rockne in football; Ty Cobb and Lou Gehrig with Ruth in baseball; "Big Bill" Tilden and Helen Wills in tennis; and Bobby Jones and Walter Hagen in golf.

The following three readings offer a glimpse of just three of the great stars: Red Grange, Babe Ruth, and Gertrude Ederle, the first woman to swim the English Channel. To match the outstanding achievements, sports writers developed a flowery style they thought would create a vivid picture for their readers.

FROM

The New York Times

SEPTEMBER 20, 1924

A flashing, red-haired youngster, running and dodging with the speed of a deer, gave 67,000 spectators jammed into the new $1,700,000 Illinois Memorial Stadium the thrill of their lives today, when Illinois vanquished Michigan, 39–14, in what probably will be the outstanding game of the 1924 gridiron season in the West.

Harold (Red) Grange, Illinois phenomenon, all-American halfback, who attained gridiron honors of the nation last season, was the dynamo that furnished the thrills. Grange doubled and redoubled his football glory in the most remarkable exhibition of running, dodging, and passing seen on any gridiron in years—an exhibition that set the dumbfounded spectators screaming with excitement.

Individually Grange scored five of Illinois' six touch-downs in a manner that left no doubt as to his ability to break through the most perfect defense. He furnished one thrill after another. On the very first kick-off Grange scooped up the ball bounding toward him on the Illinois five-yard line and raced ninety yards through the Michigan eleven for a touchdown in less than ten seconds after the starting whistle blew.

FROM

The New York Times

SEPTEMBER 8, 1927

The 1927 world's series is rapidly tottering to a lopsided finish, for yesterday George Herman Ruth hit a home run at the stadium and Herb Pennock blotted out the Pirates with three hits and the Yankees surged up the trail again to win their third straight victory before the biggest money crowd in the history of the title series. . . . The big time came in the seventh. The Yanks had the game safely stowed away and the suspense was over after six innings of sturdy batting, but the fans still stood up and demanded that Mr. Ruth get busy and do something for home and country. . . .

"A homer, Babe! Give us a homer!" ran the burden of the plea, and the big fellow pulled his cap on tighter, took a reef in his belt, dug spikes into the ground and grimly faced little Mike Cvengros, the southpaw, who had just relieved Lee Meadows. . . . Upward and onward, gaining speed and height with every foot, the little white ball

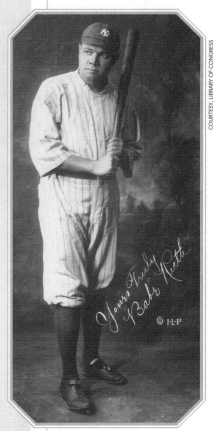

Babe Ruth.

winged with terrific speed until it dashed itself against the seats of the right-field bleachers, more than a quarter of the way up the peopled slope.

And now the populace had its homer and it stood up and gave the glad, joyous howl that must have rang out in the Roman arenas of old. . . .

Suddenly the Pirates looked very old and weary and oppressed, and life seemed to lean very heavily on their shoulders.

Gertrude Ederle's feat, achieved in 1926, was remarkable. She even beat the men's record by nearly two hours. The greatest swimmer of the age, though, was Johnny Weismuller, who later gained movie fame playing the role of Tarzan. Between 1921 and 1929, Weismuller set sixty-seven world records, never lost a freestyle race, and dominated the Olympic Games.

FROM

An Article by W. O. McGeehan

1926

If there is one woman who can make the swim, it is this girl, with the shoulders and back of Jack Dempsey and the frankest and bravest pair of eyes that ever looked into a face. She told me of her last attempt, when she swam for an hour on instinct alone, blinded, deaf, and only half conscious. She remembered only the humor of the trip. This girl keeps her even temper. I felt that I would sooner be in that tug the day she starts than at the ringside of the greatest fight or at the arena of the greatest game in the world, for this, in my opinion, is to be the greatest sports story in the world.

"Lucky" Lindbergh: The Greatest Hero

In May 1927, Charles A. Lindbergh flew his single-engine plane across the Atlantic Ocean from New York to Paris. It was a remarkable achievement. Even more remarkable was the public response. The entire world seemed suddenly to stop in wonder and in awe. Neither Europe nor the

United States had ever witnessed a celebration like the one that greeted the young aviator.

What was it that made this event so special? After all, others had flown across the Atlantic, although never before solo, and never before nonstop from New York to Paris. The fact that he did it alone was part of the magic—alone through all kinds of weather, often only a few feet above the waves, and in a plane that traveled at a speed of 100 miles per hour. Lindbergh's youth and his boyish good looks also captured people's imagination, and so did his "Aw-shucks" modesty. During his 33½-hour flight, he was equipped with only a couple of sandwiches, a map, binoculars, and a compass.

The following selection highlights the celebration that followed his successful landing.

Charles Lindbergh in 1923, before he became the world's greatest hero.

FROM

Frederick Lewis Allen's Only Yesterday

1 9 3 1

Every record for mass excitement and mass enthusiasm was smashed during the next few weeks. Nothing seemed to matter, either to the newspapers or to the people who read them, but Lindbergh and his story. The huge headlines which described Lindbergh's triumphal progress from day to day in newspapers from Maine to Oregon showed how thorough was public agreement with the somewhat extravagant dictum of the *Evening World* that Lindbergh had performed "the greatest feat of a solitary man in the records of the human race." Upon his return to the United States, a single Sunday issue of a single paper contained one hundred columns of text and pictures devoted to him. . . .

After the public welcome in New York, the Street Cleaning Department gathered up 1,800 tons of paper which had been torn up and thrown out of windows of office buildings to make a snowstorm of greeting—1,800 tons against a mere 155 tons swept up after the Armistice celebration of November 7, 1918! . . .

A Texas town was named for him, a thirteen-hundred-foot Lindbergh tower was proposed for the city of Chicago, "the largest dinner ever tendered to an individual in modern history" was consumed in his honor, and a staggering number of streets, schools, restaurants, and corporations sought to share the glory of his name.

Something that people needed was missing from their lives. And all at once Lindbergh provided it. Romance, chivalry, self-dedication—here they were, embodied in a modern Galahad.

"Flaming Youth"

For America's young men and women, the decade was a time for having fun, often by rebelling against the customs of their parents and of society. Style was an important part of this rebellion. Young men, called "Sheiks," slicked down their hair to look like movie heartthrob Rudolph Valentino as *The Sheik*. They drove expensive, speedy roadsters to football games and wore raccoon coats with a hidden flask of illegal "booze." Their dates were young women known as "Flappers," whose fashions are described in the following reading.

FROM

Preston Slosson's The Great Crusade

1930

The skirt, in the old sense of the word, disappeared altogether to be replaced by a sort of tunic or kilt barely reaching the knee. . . . Hampering petticoats were discarded as a needless impediment to free movement; silk or "rayon" stockings became practically universal . . . and for a time were often rolled at the knee, sleeves shortened or vanished, and the whole costume became a sheer and simple structure, too light to be the slightest burden. . . .

[Then] the flappers began to cut their hair. The barber shop [had been] the last refuge of masculinity in America . . . and soon there was no difference between a man's haircut and a woman's. Jewelry included several noisy bracelets and exceptionally long strands of pearls. For some, footwear consisted of unbuckled, floppy galoshes, hence, perhaps, the nickname "Flappers." They often smoked cigarettes, or pretended to, using an elegantly long holder. . . .

Cigarette advertisers took an ingenious advantage of the craze for the "boyish form"—e.g., "And now, women may enjoy a companionable smoke—at the same time slenderizing in a sensible manner. . . . Reach for a Lucky instead of a sweet." . . .

Thus the flapper of the 1920s stepped onto the stage of history, breezy, slangy, and informal in manner; slim and boyish in form; covered with silk and fur . . . and with close-fitting helmet of hair; gay, plucky, and confident.

John Held's cover art of a "flapper" and friend doing the "Charleston."

"The Lost Generation"

A number of well-known authors wrote about the disillusionment that followed World War I. Ernest Hemingway and F. Scott Fitzgerald were the most famous of these "Lost Generation" writers. The poet Gertrude Stein, an American who chose to live in France, coined the term when she said, "All of you young people who served in the war, you are the lost generation."

In *This Side of Paradise*, Fitzgerald wrote, "We were tired of Great Causes. Scarcely had the staider citizens of the republic caught their breath when the wildest of all generations which had been adolescent during the confusion of the War, danced into the limelight. . . . [We] embarked on the greatest, gaudiest spree in history."

"The Dry Decade"

In 1919, the states ratified the Eighteenth Amendment—prohibition—banning the manufacture and sale of alcoholic drinks. Congress then passed the Volstead Act to enforce the ban, and, in 1920 the nation entered "the Dry Decade."

Prohibition never worked. **Bootleggers** quickly found ways to smuggle Canadian whiskey and West Indian rum into the country. Some people made their own liquor, nicknamed "bathtub gin." The quality and safety were doubtful. Bars were closed, or served nonalcoholic drinks, but illegal clubs, called speakeasies, did a thriving business.

In the following reading, a German war hero gives his impression of how Americans got around the law.

FROM

Felix von Luckner's "Prohibition in America"

1926

In time, I learned that not everything in America was what it seemed to be. I discovered, for instance, that a spare tire could be filled with substances other than air, that one must not look too deeply into certain binoculars, and that the Teddy Bears that suddenly acquired tremendous popularity among the ladies very often had hollow metal stomachs.

"But," it might be asked, "where do all these people get the liquor?" Very simple. Prohibition has created a new, a universally respected, a well-beloved, and a very profitable occupation, that of the bootlegger who takes care of the importation of the forbidden liquor. Everyone knows this, even the powers of the government. But this profession is beloved because it is essential, and it is respected because its

bootleggers: people who smuggled whiskey, so named because early smugglers got around the law by hiding flat whiskey bottles in their boots.

pursuit is clothed with an element of danger and with a sporting risk. Now and then one is caught, that must happen pro forma, and then he must do time or, if he is wealthy enough, get someone to do time for him.

The Revival of the KKK

The original Ku Klux Klan had been formed after the Civil War by Southern whites determined to prevent the freed slaves from participating in postwar society. The KKK disappeared for several decades until it was revived by Hiram Wesley Evans in 1915.

The new Klan used methods similar to the old—white robes and hoods, cross burning, violence, and a lot of mystical mumbo jumbo. The new Klan did not limit its hatred to African Americans. Catholics, Jews, and practically all foreigners were now considered dangerous to American values. The new organization appealed to all sections of the country, especially the Midwest, achieving membership of four million by 1924.

Membership in the KKK was one way that rural Americans could express their opposition to the new, fast-paced urban life. To many farm families, it seemed that the traditions and values of the past were being undermined by outside influences. The reading that follows is Hiram Wesley Evans's statement of the Klan's purpose.

FROM

"The Klan's Fight for Americanism"

1 9 2 6

The Klan . . . has now come to speak for the great mass of Americans of the old pioneer stock. . . . These old-stock Americans are . . . a blend of various peoples of the so-called Nordic race, the race which, with all its faults, has given the

The Decline of the Klan

The success of the KKK did not last long. In the mid-1920s, the head of the Indiana Klan, David C. Stephenson, was convicted of kidnapping and murder. The incident and several financial scandals angered thousands of members. By the early 1930s, membership had dwindled to a few thousand.

world almost the whole of modern civilization. The Klan does not try to represent any people but these. . . .

The greatest achievement so far has been to formulate, focus, and gain recognition for this idea—the idea of preserving and developing America first and chiefly for the benefit of the children of the pioneers who made America. . . . When the Klan first appeared, the nation was in the confusion of sudden awakening from the lovely dream of the melting pot, disorganized and helpless before the invasion of aliens and alien ideas. After ten years of the Klan, it is in arms for defense. This is our great achievement. The second is more selfish: we have won the leadership in the movement for Americanism. Except for a few lonesome voices, almost drowned by the clamor of the alien . . . the Klan alone faces the invader. . . .

There are three great racial instincts. . . . These are the instincts of loyalty to the white race, to the traditions of America, and to the spirit of Protestantism, which has been an essential part of Americanism ever since the days of Roanoke and Plymouth Rock. They are condensed into the Klan slogan: "Native, white, Protestant supremacy."

Rural Poverty

As the nation became industrialized and urbanized, many Americans began to think of farm people as out of touch with the new world. Farm families had long been the backbone of rugged, successful Americans, the people who had led the westward expansion. By 1920, however, slick city folk began to talk of farmers as "hicks" and "hayseeds," and they became the subject of jokes and comic skits on the vaudeville stage.

Throughout the period 1900 to 1930, the way of life of many farm families had declined steadily. Thousands moved off the land every year to try for city jobs. Year after year they had seen the prices for their crops and livestock decline. The problem was that, with modern machinery and methods, the nation's farms produced so much that the price was forced downward.

Tenant farmers and **sharecroppers** suffered the most because they had no land to sell. They were constantly in debt and tried to keep working until they could break even. The following selection, a popular folk song of the 1920s and 1930s, describes the predicament.

tenant farmers: farmers who rented land for their crops.

sharecroppers: farmers who paid for use of the land by giving a share of the crop to the landowner.

FROM

'Leven-cent Cotton

C. 1925

'Leven-cent cotton, forty-cent meat,
How in the world can a poor man eat
Pray for the sunshine, 'cause it will rain
Things gettin' worse, drivin' us insane;
Built a nice house, painted it brown;
Lightnin' came along and burnt it down.
No use talkin', any man's beat
With 'leven-cent cotton and forty-cent meat.

'Leven-cent cotton, forty-cent meat,
Keep gettin' thinner 'cause we don't eat;
Tried to raise peas, tried to raise beans;
All we can raise is turnip greens.
No corn in the crib, no chicks in the yard,
No meat in the smokehouse, no tubs full of lard;
No use talkin', any man's beat
With 'leven-cent cotton and forty-cent meat.

'Leven-cent cotton, forty-cent meat,
How in the world can a poor man eat?
Mule's in the barn, no crop's laid by,
Corncrib empty and the cow's gone dry.
Well water's low, nearly out of sight,
Can't take a bath on a Saturday night.
No use talkin', any man's beat
With 'leven-cent cotton and forty-cent meat.

Between 1920 and 1924, banks took over more than 100,000 farms because the families couldn't pay their debts. The farm, equipment, and livestock were usually sold by auction.

The "Jazz Age"

The novelist F. Scott Fitzgerald called the 1920s the "Jazz Age." He meant the label to apply to the fast-paced lifestyle of the period as well as the musical form of jazz. Jazz was one of many African American gifts to music. It built on themes from gospel music, the blues, and ragtime; in its frenzied speed and improvisation, it was also a revolt against tradition and custom. Jazz had its origins in the South, in New Orleans and other towns, then spread rapidly north, especially to the Harlem section of New York City. In the following selection, James A. Rogers describes the social aspects of jazz.

FROM

James A. Rogers, "Jazz at Home"

1925

What after all is this new thing, that, condemned in certain quarters, enthusiastically welcomed in others, has nonchalantly gone on until it ranks with the movie and the dollar as the foremost exponent of modern Americanism? Jazz isn't music merely, it is a spirit that can express itself in almost anything. The true spirit of jazz is a joyous revolt from convention, custom, authority, boredom, even sorrow—from everything that would confine the soul of man and hinder its riding free on the air. The Negroes who invented it called their songs the "Blues," and they weren't capable of satire or deception. Jazz was their explosive attempt to cast off the blues and be happy, carefree happy even in the midst of sordidness and sorrow. And that is why it has been such a balm for modern ennui, and has become a safety valve for modern machine-ridden and convention-bound society. It is the revolt of the emotions against repression.

The "Harlem Renaissance"

In the Harlem section of New York City, two cultures came together when wealthy white Americans came to Harlem to hear the great jazz bands and solo performers. Duke Ellington, through his band and his musical compositions, helped gain worldwide recognition of the new musical form. Solo performers like Louis Armstrong had a popularity that continued through the 1900s.

In addition to being a gathering spot for jazz musicians and audiences, Harlem was also the scene for a great flowering of African American literature and art. Langston Hughes was one of the youthful leaders of this Harlem Renaissance. The selection that follows is from his first book of poetry, *Weary Blues*.

Langston Hughes's "Lament for Dark Peoples"

1926

I was a red man one time,
But the white men came.
I was a black man, too,
But the white men came.

They drove me out of the forest.
They took me away from the jungles.
I lost my trees.
I lost my silver moons.

Now they've caged me
In the circus of civilization.
Now I herd with the many—
Caged in the circus of civilization.

Langston Hughes, poet of the "Harlem Renaissance."

Fads and Crazes

The wild decade of the 1920s was also a time of fads and crazes. Millions of people worked endless crossword puzzles and every newspaper and magazine presented new ones. People played bridge just as avidly, and for others a favorite pastime was the game mah-jongg. Marathon dance contests could last forty hours or more as couples struggled to stay on their feet for prize money.

Americans were also fond of stunts. Daredevils performed feats like hitting a golf ball from the top of an airplane several hundred feet in the air, or flying upside down in an open-cockpit plane. Huge crowds also stood for hours to watch an ex-boxer named Shipwreck Kelly sit on a tiny perch on top of a flagpole. As the following selection shows, the flagpole-sitting fad hit young people as well.

FROM

"The Child Stylelites of Baltimore"

1929

It all started when, a few weeks ago, a curious fellow known as Shipwreck Kelly, who goes from city to city demonstrating the hardihood of the American posterior by sitting for extended periods on flagpoles, visited the conservative city of Baltimore and "put on a sitting." During his protracted stay aloft, which was long enough to break the world's record for this particular form of virtuosity, Shipwreck attracted large crowds . . . and the celebration attending his eventual descent was a demonstration of the ease with which almost any form of imbecility becomes important in these States. Inevitably there was a juvenile aspirant to Shipwreck's fame. Boys from time immemorial have wanted to be locomotive engineers, bareback raiders, and major generals. Their heroes are, quite naturally, those who cause the most excitement. It was no great surprise, therefore, when one read in the Baltimore newspapers the modest announcement that Avon Freeman, fifteen, had mounted a flagpole and would sit there until he had broken what might be considered the "juvenile record." When he had sat for ten days, ten hours, ten minutes and ten seconds, he decided that the "juvenile record" in this field had been broken, and he came down. . . .

The mayor of Baltimore congratulated the boy for showing "America's pioneer spirit."

PART V

THE GREAT DEPRESSION AND THE NEW DEAL

For many Americans, the 1920s had been a joyful, often zany ride. The majority of families enjoyed an increasingly comfortable standard of living. They owned their own homes, and many enjoyed such conveniences as a family car, a radio, a refrigerator, and a variety of other appliances and gadgets. There seemed no reason that this wave of prosperity shouldn't roll on indefinitely.

But it turned out there were many reasons the good times could not continue. The beginning of the end came in 1929 when the stock market crashed. That sudden crash touched off a chain reaction—banks closed, savings were wiped out, factories laid off workers, and unemployment lines grew.

From 1929 to 1932 the nation plunged deeper into depression. The income of U.S. families dropped by more than half; 86,000 businesses failed and millions were out of work, while those who still had jobs saw their wages drop by 60 percent. And that was just the beginning. These years became known as the Great Depression because of how deep the decline was and how long it lasted. Only the approach of World War II, twelve years after the crash, finally ended the Depression.

In March 1933, Democrat Franklin D. Roosevelt entered the White House, launching an avalanche of projects to lift the United States out of the hard times. FDR's New Deal gave Americans hope, and many of the programs relieved suffering and brought desperately needed improvement in economic and social conditions. Even the New Deal was not a cure-all, however, and the country stumbled through the closing years of the 1930s.

From Boom to Bust

In the summer of 1929, the economist Roger Babson was one of the few people who predicted both the crash and the Depression. "Sooner or later a crash is coming," Babson wrote, "and it may be terrific. Factories will shut down . . . men will be thrown out of work . . . the vicious circle will get in full swing and the result will be a serious depression."

As the 1920s drew to a close, a few people saw that there was trouble ahead. One sign of trouble was that the stock market was dangerously overheated. In the past, people had bought stocks as a long-term investment. They received annual dividends on their stock—their share of the company's profits—and, over time, as the company grew, the value of the stock increased.

In the fast-paced 1920s, however, people began to see stocks as a quick way to wealth. The value of stocks was climbing at a record rate. As more and more people bought, they pushed the price up even faster. Then, by 1927, people began buying on margin: they paid a small down payment for, say, 100 shares of General Motors stock, then borrowed the rest of the price from the stock broker. When the value of that stock increased over the next few months, the investor could sell and pay off the broker from the profits.

For some investors, the stock market and margin buying were like an exciting game. Newspapers had daily stories of quick wealth: a taxi driver turned a $2,000 investment into a $17,000 jackpot; or a beauty parlor technician made $20,000 in a little over a year.

But what would happen if everyone decided to sell at the same time? How could brokers collect from all the people who had borrowed? If the price of stocks began to fall rapidly, how much would you lose when you sold those shares? Few people thought about these questions until September and October 1929.

New York Times headline,
the day after "Black Tuesday."

The rapid selling of stocks started on Thursday, October 24. The market rallied on Friday, but then on Monday, October 28, people owning stock panicked and started an avalanche of selling that continued on "Black Tuesday," October 29. In the following selection, the journalist Jonathan Norton Leonard describes the scene on Wall Street at the time of the crash.

FROM

Jonathan Norton Leonard's Eyewitness Report

OCTOBER 1929

That night [Monday, October 28] Wall Street was lit up like a Christmas tree. Restaurants, barber shops, and speakeasies were open and doing a roaring business. Messenger boys and runners raced through the streets whooping and singing at

Stock Market Losses

The decline in stock prices continued far past Black Tuesday. General Motors, for example, one of the nation's steadiest corporations, saw its stock drop in value from $70 a share in 1928 to about $8 in 1931. So an investor with, say 1,000 shares, had stock worth $70,000 in 1928; by 1931, it was worth only $8,000—a loss of $62,000!

the top of their lungs. Slum children invaded the district to play with balls of ticker tape. Well-dressed gentlemen fell asleep in lunch counters. All the downtown hotels, rooming houses, even flophouses were full of financial employees who usually slept in the Bronx. It was probably Wall Street's worst night. Not only had the day been bad, but everybody down to the youngest office boy had a pretty good idea of what was going to happen tomorrow.

The morning papers were black with the story of the Monday smash. Except for rather feeble hopes that the great banks would step into the gap, they had no heart for cheerful headlines. In the inside pages, however, the sunshine chorus continued as merry as ever. Bankers said that heavy buying had been sighted on the horizon. Brokers were loud with "technical" reasons why the decline could not continue.

The next day, Tuesday, the 29th of October, was the worst of all. In the first half hour 3,259,800 shares were traded, almost a full day's work for the laboring machinery of the Exchange. The selling pressure was wholly without precedent. It was coming from everywhere. The wires to other cities were jammed with frantic orders to sell. So were the cables, radio, and telephones to Europe and the rest of the world. Buyers were few, sometimes wholly absent. . . .

This was real panic. It was what the banks had prevented on Thursday, had slowed on Monday. Now they were helpless. . . .

When the closing bell rang, the great bull market was dead and buried. 16,410,000 shares had changed hands. Leading stocks had lost as much as 77 percent of their peak value. . . . Not only the little speculators, but the lordly, experienced big traders had been wiped out by the violence of the crash, and the whole financial structure of the nation had been shaken to its foundations. Many bankers and brokers were doubtful about their own solvency, for their accounting systems had broken down. The truth was buried beneath a mountain of scribbled paper which would require several days of solid work to clear away.

Hard Times

The stock market crash was just the tip of the economic iceberg. Business was at a standstill and thousands of factories were forced to lay off workers or shut down completely. The need to pay off loans caused a rush on banks; many banks ran out of cash and closed their doors, often permanently, and several million people lost their life savings. By 1933, the worst year of the Depression, one out of every four workers was unemployed.

In the early 1930s, there were few cushions to protect people against such hardships. There were no unemployment benefits, no social security, no health insurance. Except for a few local charities, people had nowhere to turn for help.

The selections that follow describe conditions in the early 1930s: a rather typical morning for an unemployed worker in New Haven, Connecticut, and a description of a shantytown in a garbage dump in Youngstown, Ohio.

FROM

The Journal of E. W. Bakke

APRIL 1933

April 27

Up at seven, cup of coffee, and off to Sargent's. Like to be there when the gang comes to work, the lucky devils. Employment manager not in. Waited in his outer office. . . . Three others waiting, two reporting for compensation. Other one laid off two weeks ago and said he called at office every day. He inquired what I was doing and when I said "looking for work" he laughed. "You never work here? No? What chance you think you got when 400 like me who belong here [are] out?" Employment manager showed up at 9:30. I had waited two hours. My time has no value. A pleasant fellow told me in a kind but snappy way business was very bad. What about the future; would he take my name? Said he referred only to the present. Nothing more for me to say, so left. Two more had drifted into office. Suppose they got the same story. Must be a lot of men in New Haven that have heard it by now.

FROM

Charles R. Walker's "Relief and Revolution"

1 9 3 2

Some of [the shanties] are caves with tin roofs, but all of them blend with the place, for they are constructed out of it. From 150 to 200 men live in shanties. The place is called by its inhabitants—Hooverville.

I went forward and talked to the men; they showed me their houses. These vary greatly from mere caves covered with a piece of tin, to weather-proof shanties built of packing boxes and equipped with a stolen window-frame or an improved door. Some have beds and one or two a kitchen stove rescued from the junk heap, though most of the men cook in communal fashion over a fire shielded by bricks in the open.

The inhabitants were not, as one might expect, outcasts or "untouchables," or even hoboes in the American sense; they were men without jobs. Life is sustained by begging, eating at the city soup kitchens, or earning a quarter by polishing an automobile—enough to bring home bacon and bread. Eating "at home" is preferred. The location of the town also has its commissary advantage; men take part of their food from the garbage house. This I entered; the stench of decaying food is appalling. Here I found that there were more women than men—gathering food for their families.

Hooverizing

Americans displayed their anger at the president by attaching the name Hoover to symbols of their suffering. Shantytowns were called Hoovervilles for that reason. Similarly, the newspapers used for warmth when sleeping on park benches were called Hoover blankets.

Hoover's Basic Decency

President Hoover was not unsympathetic to the suffering. His fame, in fact, had been based in large part on his efforts to save millions from starvation during World War I. And he believed in private and community charity, but he did not want the federal government simply to give money to the needy. He said that kind of "dole" would destroy freedom and initiative. Hoover also failed to see how deep the Depression was or how long-lasting. When a citizens' group appealed to him for federal aid in 1930, he said, "You have come sixty days too late. The depression is over."

A "Hooverville" in Seattle, 1937.

FDR Launches the New Deal

By 1932, Americans were eager for a change. Democrat Franklin Delano Roosevelt easily won the presidential election over Hoover, with an electoral vote of 472 to 59. The vote was as much anti-Hoover as it was pro-FDR, because people were not really sure what Roosevelt planned to do. Kansas editor William Allen White expressed the uncertainty felt by many: "No one knows his heart and few have seen behind the masking smile that wreathes his face. We are putting our hands in a grab-bag. Heaven only knows what we shall pull out."

Roosevelt's plans were unknown, but his name and personality were familiar. Born into an aristocratic New York State family, Roosevelt was a distant cousin of President Theodore Roosevelt and, in 1905, he married another distant cousin, Anna Eleanor Roosevelt. He enjoyed politics and served under President Woodrow Wilson as assistant secretary of the navy during World War I. He was the Democratic nominee for vice president in the 1920 election. A year after that defeat, Roosevelt was stricken with polio (infantile paralysis), which left his legs permanently paralyzed.

Roosevelt was thirty-nine years old and his political career seemed over. But his own fierce determination and the great energy and support of his wife, Eleanor, enabled him to make a remarkable political comeback. He built up his upper body strength so that he could pull himself to his feet and stand with the help of heavy steel braces. News reporters and editors remained respectful, saying little about his crippled condition and printing no photographs of his braces or wheelchair.

In 1928, Roosevelt was elected governor of New York, won reelection in 1930, and then won the presidency in 1932. During the presidential campaign, his plans for ending the Depression often seemed vague, but it was clear that he promised action and what he called "a new deal for the American people."

In the following selection, from FDR's inaugural address, the president describes the challenge.

The "Hundred Days" and "Fireside Chats"

After taking office in March 1933, Roosevelt kept the Congress in Special Session and delivered message after message to be translated into new programs. He also made other decisions by Executive Order, like a "Bank Holiday," which closed all banks until government bank examiners could decide which ones were strong enough to reopen. This flood of actions from March to June became known as the "Hundred Days."

From time to time, the president delivered a "Fireside Chat"—an informal radio address—to explain his actions to the people, and this proved to be one of the ways Roosevelt maintained his great popularity. The technique had been followed by several later presidents.

FROM

Roosevelt's Inaugural Address

MARCH 4, 1933

I am certain that my fellow Americans expect that on my induction into the Presidency I will address them with a candor and a decision which the present situation of our Nation impels. . . . Nor need we shrink from honestly facing conditions in our country today. This great Nation will endure as it has endured, will revive and will prosper. So, first of all, let me assert my firm belief that the only thing we have to fear is fear itself—nameless, unreasoning, unjustified terror which paralyzes needed efforts to convert retreat into advance. . . .

Our distress comes from no failure of substance. . . . Plenty is at our doorstep, but a generous use of it languishes in the very sight of the supply. Primarily this is because rulers of the exchange of mankind's goods have failed through their own stubbornness and their own incompetence, have admitted their failure, and have abdicated. . . . They have no vision, and where there is no vision the people perish. . . . The money changers have fled from their high seats in the temple of our civilization. . . .

This Nation asks for action, and action now.

Our greatest primary task is to put people to work. This is no unsolvable problem if we face it wisely and courageously. It can be accomplished in part by direct recruiting by the Government itself, treating the task as we would treat the emergency of war. . . . We must endeavor to provide a better use of the land for those best fitted for the land. . . . We require . . . safeguards against a return of the evils of the old order. . . . Our Constitution is so simple and practical that it is possible always to meet extraordinary needs. . . .

I am prepared under my constitutional duty to recommend the measures that a stricken Nation in the midst of a

Will Rogers on the Hundred Days

The nation's most popular humorist, Will Rogers, kept Americans smiling through the darkest days. Part Cherokee and all cowboy, and speaking in his easy Oklahoma drawl while twirling a lasso, he said of the Hundred Days, "The whole country is with him. Even if what he does is wrong they are with him. Just so he does something. If he burned down the Capitol, we would cheer and say, 'Well, we at least got a fire started anyhow!'"

stricken world may require. These measures, or such other measures as the Congress may build out of its experience and wisdom, I shall seek, within my constitutional authority, to bring to speedy adoption.

Frances Perkins

Frances Perkins had been a social worker during the progressive movement in the early 1900s. Roosevelt named her to his cabinet as secretary of labor, the first woman to hold a cabinet-level position. She agreed to accept the position only if the president agreed to propose a program of social security. Roosevelt willingly agreed and, in his second term, he placed Perkins in charge of formulating the Social Security Act, which continues today to provide unemployment benefits to people who are out of work, as well as pensions to retired workers and the disabled. Secretary Perkins served in FDR's government for twelve years.

FROM

Frances Perkins's Memoirs

1946

When Franklin Roosevelt and his administration began their work in Washington in March 1933, the New Deal was not a plan with form and content. It was a happy phrase he had coined during the campaign, and its value was psychological. It made people feel better, and in that terrible period of depression they needed to feel better.

As Roosevelt described it, the "new deal" meant that the forgotten person, the little person, the person nobody knew much about, was going to be dealt better cards to play with.

The idea was not specific; it was general, but it was

potent. On Roosevelt's part it was truly and profoundly felt. He understood that the suffering of the depression had fallen with terrific impact upon the people least able to bear it. He knew that the rich had been hit hard too, but at least they had something left. But the little merchant, the small householder, and the home owner, the farmer who worked the soil, the person who worked for wages—these people were desperate. And Roosevelt saw them as principal citizens of the United States.

Work Programs

One of the major goals of the New Deal was to put as many people to work as possible, and one of the most successful of these work relief programs was the Civilian Conservation Corps, or CCC. Over a ten-year period the CCC put more than two million young men to work in the nation's parks and forests. They made camping grounds and picnic areas, planted trees, fought forest fires, and lived in army-style camps. Part of their pay was sent home or placed in bank accounts. Thousands of young men who had not known what it was like to earn money or to eat three healthy meals a day found new hope in the CCC. In the following selection, Luther Wandall describes his experience.

FROM

Luther Wandall's "A Negro in the CCC"

1935

According to instructions, I went Monday morning at 8 o'clock to Pier I, North River. There were more than 1,000 boys standing about the pier. . . .

The colored boys were a goodly sprinkling of the whole. A few middle-aged men were in evidence. These, it turned out, were going as cooks. A good many Spaniards and Italians were about. A good natured, lively, crowd, typical of New York. . . . We answered questions, signed papers, and then a group of us marched over to the U.S. Army headquarters on Whitehall Street in charge of an Army officer.

Here we stripped for a complete physical examination. Then we were grouped into busloads. . . .

We reached Camp Dix [New Jersey] about 7:30 that evening. As we rolled up in front of headquarters an officer came out to the bus and told us: "You will double-time as you leave this bus, remove your hat when you hit the door, and when you are asked questions, answer 'Yes, sir,' and 'No, sir.'"

When my record was taken at Pier I a "C" was placed on it. When the busloads were made up at Whitehall street an officer reported as follows: "35, 8 colored." But until now there had been no distinction made.

Unemployed young men arrive at a CCC project in Tennessee.

We were taken to permanent camp on a site rich in Colonial and Revolutionary history, in the upper South. This camp was a dream compared with Camp Dix. There [was] plenty to eat, and we slept in barracks instead of tents. An excellent recreation hall, playground, and other facilities.

I am still in this camp. At the "rec" [recreation room] we have a radio, a piano, a store called a "canteen," a rack of the leading New York papers, white and colored, as well as some from elsewhere. There is a little library and a variety of books and magazines. All sports are encouraged. We have a baseball team, boxing squad, etc. An orchestra has been formed, and classes in various arts and crafts.

During the first week we did no work outside camp, but

only hiked, drilled, and exercised. Since then we have worked five days a week, eight hours a day. Our bosses are local men, southerners, but on the whole I have found nothing to complain of. The work varies, but is always healthy, outdoor labor. As the saying goes, it's a great life, if only you don't weaken!

The Dust Bowl

Farm families on the Great Plains had relied on cash crops, especially wheat and corn, since the 1880s. Desperate for cash income, they planted the same crops in the same fields year after year. They cut down trees and plowed up gardens and lawns to plant still more. By 1930, with nothing to hold the soil in place, millions of acres of farmland west of the Mississippi River were turning to dust.

In 1933, the first dust storm hit when winds lifted an estimated three hundred million tons of topsoil into the air. People called the storm a "black blizzard." As it moved east, it blotted out the sun in Chicago, and left a thin layer of dust on everything in Albany and then in Boston. The black blizzards were repeated through 1934, 1935, and 1936. An estimated 2,500,000 people were displaced by the Dust Bowl conditions in a region stretching from the Dakotas and Montana in the North to New Mexico, Oklahoma, and Texas in the South. Many took to the road, driving beat-up Fords—or walking—often heading for year-round farm work in California.

An outstanding journalist named Lorena Hickok was in South Dakota when the first black blizzard struck on November 11, 1933. Hickok was just starting an amazing fact-finding journey for Harry Hopkins, Roosevelt's director of the Federal Emergency Relief Administration. Her two-year tour took her to thirty-two states. While her reports normally went to Hopkins, the letter used in the following selection was to Hickok's close friend Eleanor Roosevelt, the President's wife.

Hickok's letter is followed by an excerpt from John Steinbeck's famous novel *The Grapes of Wrath,* about farm families trying to escape the Dust Bowl and get to California.

Dust Bowl Humor

Although these farm families seemed to have lost everything, they kept their sense of humor. Some examples:

- "I kinda like settin' on my porch and watchin' the neighbors' farms blow by."
- "Well, we haven't lost everything. The wind blew the whole damn ranch out of state, but we ain't lost everything—we still have the mortgage."
- "I'll plow next week. I reckon the farm'll blow back from Oklahoma by then."

FROM

Lorena Hickok's Letter to Eleanor Roosevelt

NOVEMBER 1933

I thought I'd already seen about everything in the way of desolation, discomfort, and misery that could exist, right here in South Dakota. Well, it seems that I hadn't. Today's little treat was a dust storm. And I mean a dust storm!

It started to blow last night. All night the wind howled and screamed and sobbed around the windows.

When I got up, at 7:30 this morning, the sky seemed to be clear, but you couldn't see the sun! There was a queer brown haze—only right above was the sky clear. And the wind was blowing a gale. It kept on blowing, harder and harder. And the haze kept mounting in the sky. By the time we had finished breakfast and were ready to start out, about 9, the sun was only a lighter spot in the dust that filled the sky like a brown fog.

We drove only a few miles and had to turn back. It got worse and worse—rapidly. You couldn't see a foot ahead of the car by the time we got back, and we had a time getting back! It was like driving through a fog, only worse, for there was that damnable wind. It seemed as though the car would be blown right off the road any minute. When we stopped we had to put on the emergency brake. The wind, behind us, actually moved the car. It was a truly terrifying experience. It was as though we had left the earth. We were being whirled off into space in a vast, impenetrable cloud of brown dust.

A man and a boy head for cover in an Oklahoma dust storm, 1936; one of Arthur Rothstein's famous photos.

COURTESY, LIBRARY OF CONGRESS

They had the street lights on when we finally groped our way back into town. They stayed on the rest of the day. By noon the sun wasn't even a light spot in the sky any more. You couldn't see it at all. It was so dark, and the dust was so thick that you couldn't see across the street. I was lying on the bed reading the paper and glanced up—the window looked black, just as it does at night. I was terrified, for a moment. It seemed like the end of the world.

It didn't stop blowing until sundown, and now the dust has begun to settle. If you look straight up, you can see some stars!

FROM

John Steinbeck's The Grapes of Wrath

1939

The cars of the migrant people crawled out of the side roads onto the great cross-country highway, and they took the migrant way to the West. In the daylight they scuttled like bugs to the westward; and as the dark caught them, they clustered like bugs near to shelter and to water. And because they were lonely and perplexed, because they had all come from a place of sadness and worry and defeat, and because they were all going to a new mysterious place, they huddled together; they talked together, they shared their lives, their food, and the things they hoped for in the new country. Thus it might be that one family camped near a spring, and another camped for the spring and for the company, and a third because two families had pioneered the place and found it good. And when the sun went down, perhaps twenty families and twenty cars were there.

In the evening a strange thing happened: the twenty families became one family, the children were the children

The Power of The Grapes of Wrath

John Steinbeck's novel followed the fictional Joad family on their trek to California. They were called "Okies"—a nickname applied to most of the migrants because many came from Oklahoma, even though they came from several other states as well. The book had a powerful influence in creating sympathy for these stricken farm families and in gaining popular support for the government's programs.

of all. The loss of home became one loss, and the golden time in the West was one dream. And it might be that a sick child threw despair into the hearts of twenty families, of a hundred people; that a birth there in a tent kept a hundred quiet and awestruck through the night and filled a hundred people with the birth-joy in the morning. A family which the night before had been lost and fearful might search its goods to find a present for a new baby. In the evening, sitting about the fires, the twenty were one.

Creating a Documentary Record

During the Depression, a growing number of Americans became interested in documenting the events of these turbulent years. Sociologists, journalists, and government workers were everywhere—interviewing people and compiling evidence of how people's lives were affected by the huge changes in the nation's economic and social life.

One special recording group was part of the government's Farm Security Administration, or FSA. Called the Historical Section, this group was to document conditions in the nation's farming regions. The Historical Section's director, Roy Emerson Stryker, put together a team of brilliant young photographers, including Dorothea Lange, Walker Evans, Arthur Rothstein, and the artist Ben Shahn. From 1935 through 1938, this outstanding group produced a file of roughly 270,000 photographs.

The photos were supplied to newspapers and magazines, creating a running account of the need for New Deal programs and the changes those programs were bringing about. In terms of history, the Historical Section's work provides us today with an amazing pictorial record of the faces and events of the Depression years.

Stryker insisted that the photographers find scenes that showed strength as well as hard times. When someone suggested that all the pictures were depressing, Stryker said, "I say look again. You see the set of that

Dorothea Lange's photograph of a migrant farm wife in California.

COURTESY, LIBRARY OF CONGRESS

chin. You see the way that mother stands. You see the straight line of that man's shoulders. You see something in those faces that transcends misery."

Eleanor Roosevelt: The President's "Legs and Ears"

Throughout his presidency, Roosevelt depended on his wife, Eleanor, to be his "legs and ears." She traveled constantly, bringing back information that the president relied on. In cabinet meetings, he often presented the information with the introduction, "The Missus says. . . . "

Eleanor Roosevelt first proved her incredible courage and determination after Franklin was stricken with polio. In addition to helping him through his long and painful recovery, she raised five children and kept his political career alive with numerous speeches and public appearances. After FDR's election to the presidency, Eleanor became the most active first lady in history, and often the most controversial because she became a spokesperson for the rights of women, African Americans, and other groups that could not participate fully in the life of the nation. Following her husband's death in 1945, she became a delegate to the United Nations, where she played a central role in creating the UN Declaration of Human Rights.

In the following selection, Mrs. Roosevelt recalls some of the personal obstacles she had to overcome.

FROM

Eleanor Roosevelt's On My Own

1958

I was often terrified by the notion that I would never amount to anything and that I was so homely that no man would want to marry me. These fears remained with me for a long time. . . . I was afraid of doing anything myself. It was many years before I had the confidence to drive a car. It was even hard for me to give an opinion. . . .

Speaking in public was one of the most difficult tasks I had to contemplate. . . . I forced myself to overcome [the fears] because there was no way to avoid it. . . . By the time of Franklin's election to the presidency, I felt more comfortable at the microphone. . . . Another thing that helped me during those White House years was my great concern for those who were suffering. As I wrote to a friend, I had moments of real terror when I thought we might be losing an entire generation of young people. I was now in a position to do something to help, and my early fears vanished like bad dreams.

Eleanor Roosevelt's Social Protest

In 1939, Marian Anderson, one of the nation's greatest concert singers, who also happened to be African American, was denied use of a concert hall in Washington, D.C., owned by the DAR (Daughters of the American Revolution). Mrs. Roosevelt publicly resigned from the organization and, with the help of Harold Ickes, head of the Public Works Administration (PWA), arranged to have Miss Anderson give an Easter concert from the steps of the Lincoln Memorial. The Roosevelts then persuaded her to sing at the White House for the king and queen of England. Mrs. Roosevelt said the royal couple "would want to hear the music that above all else we could call our own."

Songs of the Depression

A number of young folk singers produced outstanding songs during the Depression, usually by writing out of their own experiences with hard times. Woody Guthrie, who became one of the most famous, was an Okie who joined the long trek to California. "When the black dust hit our country," he said later, "I was among the first to blow. When it cleared off again, I woke up with a guitar in one hand and a road map in the other." The following selection was one of Guthrie's earliest.

FROM

Woody Guthrie's "So Long (It's Been Good to Know Yuh)"

C. 1937

I've sung this song, but I'll sing it again,
Of the people I've met, and the places I've seen,
Of some of the troubles that bothered my mind,
And a lot of good people that I've left behind. So it's

So long, it's been good to know yuh,
So long, it's been good to know yuh,
So long, it's been good to know yuh,
What a long time since I've been home,
And I got to be drifting along.

I walked down the street to the grocery store,
It was crowded with people both rich and both poor,
I asked the man how his butter was sold,
He said, one pound of butter for two pounds of gold; I said:

So long, etc.

I went to your family and asked them for you,
They all said take her, oh, take her, please do!
She can't cook or sew and she won't scrub your floor,
So I put on my hat and tiptoed out the door, saying:

So long, etc.

WPA and the Arts

Artists, composers, playwrights, and dancers might have found the hard times overwhelming if it hadn't been for the WPA—the Works Progress Administration. This program, one of the largest New Deal measures, reflected Roosevelt's belief in giving people meaningful work. He said that the goal was to "preserve not only the bodies of the unemployed . . . but also their self-respect, their self-confidence and courage and determination." From 1935 to 1942, WPA director Harry Hopkins spent the incredible sum of $11 billion, and more than 85 percent of it went for salaries. Thousands of WPA artists painted murals and posters, put on stage plays and concerts, and gave impromptu performances on street corners.

World's Fairs

When a world's fair opened in Chicago in May 1933, many predicted that few people would be interested in futuristic buildings or daring amusement rides. Instead, the "Century of Progress Exposition" was a great success, drawing more than twenty million visitors. People were awed by special effects, like having a faint beam of light from the star Arcturus move the switch that turned on the lights.

Six years later, the New York World's Fair was also a great success. Called the "World of Tomorrow," it gave people a glimpse of possible futures, like riding on General Motors's twisting futuristic highway that required no steering.

Fun for Kids

A variety of new entertainment forms offered enjoyment for kids. Comic strips had been popular in newspapers for some twenty years, for example, but the 1930s introduced *Action Comics* and a new hero—Superman. Dozens of other comic books followed. Also popular were "Big-little" books—fat, square cubes with text on one side of a page and a cartoon drawing on the other. Walt Disney provided a new form of family entertainment with his feature-length animations like *Snow White and the Seven Dwarfs*. Movie musicals were also popular, especially *The Wizard of Oz*.

Radio programs offered exciting dramas such as "The Lone Ranger" and "The Shadow." Many of these shows invited listeners to send away for badges, secret-code rings, and other paraphernalia. Movie serials were also popular—fifteen-minute dramas shown on Saturday afternoons, always ending in yet another cliff-hanger.

All of these entertainment forms spelled out the important values of the times, especially playing fair, being honest, and having faith in the American way of life.

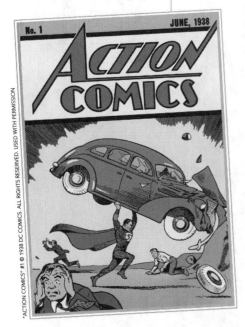

Superman—the first of the superheroes.

PART VI

THE SECOND WORLD WAR

During the 1920s and 1930s, military dictators came to power in several countries, notably Germany, Italy, and Japan. These were fascist dictatorships, in which all of a country's institutions were controlled by the government, including schools, newspapers, radio, and banks. In Germany, control was exercised by Adolf Hitler and his National Socialist, or Nazi, party; Mussolini's Fascist party controlled Italy's institutions; and in Japan, the military kept a tight control on all aspects of life. These were harsh regimes, in which all opposition was ruthlessly crushed and basic human rights were suppressed.

The American people generally chose to ignore what was happening in other parts of the world, insisting on the strict policy of isolationism established after World War I. The United States even closed its doors to immigrants, passing laws in the 1920s that limited immigration to a trickle, mostly from western Europe.

By the late 1930s the three "Axis" powers—Germany, Italy, and Japan—had begun campaigns of conquest. Many Americans became increasingly alarmed, including President Roosevelt. The majority of the people, however, and most members of Congress, were firmly opposed to any U.S. involvement. For several years, the president battled the isolationists in Congress until December 7, 1941, when Japan attacked the American naval base at Pearl Harbor in Hawaii, plunging the nation into World War II.

The war years, 1941 to 1945, showed the United States at its best. The voices you'll encounter in this section, covering both the homefront and the battlefronts, will provide evidence of why this has been called "the best generation."

The Approach of War

Most Americans were confident that the United States could stay out of the war, until the spring of 1940, when everything changed. In a matter of weeks, the powerful German war machine stormed across much of Europe, conquering nation after nation, including France. This was the German "Blitzkrieg," or "Lightning War." By summer, only England stood between Hitler and total domination of Europe. As German bombers began nightly raids over England to prepare for invasion, the American people finally realized that the United States was not immune. They listened when English prime minister Winston Churchill warned that, if England fell, "then the whole world, including the United States . . . will sink into the abyss of a new Dark Age."

Americans felt the war coming closer. One indication was the draft, requiring all males between the ages of eighteen and forty-five to register for military service. Movie newsreels gave audiences visual images of the bombing raids over England, and a sense of immediacy was provided by the nightly radio reports from London by the radio journalist Edward R. Murrow. The reading that follows is from one of Murrow's broadcasts, during which listeners heard the background sounds of exploding bombs, antiaircraft fire, and sirens.

FROM

Edward R. Murrow's Radio Broadcast

OCTOBER 10, 1940

This is London, ten minutes before five in the morning. Tonight's raid has been widespread. London is again the main target. Bombs have been reported from more than fifty districts. Raiders have been over Wales in the west, the Midlands, Liverpool, the Southwest, and Northeast. So far as London is concerned, the outskirts appear to have suffered the heaviest pounding. The attack has decreased in intensity since the moon faded from the sky. . . .

A German bomber came boring down the river. We could see his exhaust trail like a pale ribbon stretched straight across the sky. Half a mile downstream there were two eruptions and then a third, close together. The first two looked like some giant had thrown a huge basket of flaming golden oranges high in the air. The third was just a balloon of fire enclosed in black smoke above the housetops. The observer . . . reached for his night glasses, took one quick look, picked up his telephone, and said, "Two high explosives and one oil bomb," and named the street where they had fallen. . . . There was peace and quiet inside [the observation tower] for twenty minutes. Then a shower of incendiaries [fire bombs] came down in the distance.

The Isolationists

Several million Americans remained firmly opposed to entering the war or even sending aid to England. This strong belief in keeping the United States isolated remained through 1940 and 1941. The America First Committee organized huge rallies at Madison Square Garden in New York City, where one of the most popular speakers was the famed aviator Charles A.

Lindbergh. Lindbergh had seen Germany's military buildup firsthand and he was most impressed by the air power. He felt that the United States was totally unprepared for war and, if war came, the nation would lose. He also believed that the country was protected from invasion by the oceans. The next selection is from one of his speeches. Lindbergh was severely criticized for his stand, but, when war came, he fully supported the U.S. war effort and even secretly flew fifty combat missions in the Pacific.

FROM

Charles A. Lindbergh's Speech before the America First Committee

MAY 1941

I have said before, and I will say again, that I believe it will be a tragedy to the entire world if the British Empire collapses. That is one of the main reasons why I opposed this war before it was declared, and why I have constantly advocated a negotiated peace. I did not feel that England and France had a reasonable chance of winning. France has now been defeated; and despite the propaganda and confusion of recent months, it is now obvious that England is losing the war. I believe this is realized even by the British Government. But they have one last desperate plan remaining. They hope that they may be able to persuade us to send another American Expeditionary Force to Europe and to share with England militarily, as well as financially, the fiasco of this war.

It is not only our right, but it is our obligation as American citizens to look at this war objectively and to weigh our chances for success if we should enter it. I have attempted to do this, especially from the standpoint of aviation; and I have been forced to the conclusion that we cannot win this war for England, regardless of how much assistance we send. . . .

The United States is better situated from a military standpoint than any other nation in the world. Even in our present condition of unpreparedness no foreign power is in a position to invade us today. If we concentrate on our own defenses and build the strength that this nation should maintain, no foreign army will ever attempt to land on American shores.

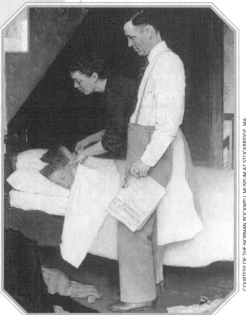

Norman Rockwell's "Freedom from Fear," part of his Four Freedoms series.

In his 1941 State of the Union message, President Roosevelt spoke of four Freedoms that should be available to all the world's people: freedom of speech, freedom of religion, freedom from want, and freedom from fear of foreign aggression. In 1943, Norman Rockwell (1894–1978), the popular illustrator and artist, completed a series of four paintings that interpreted the four in terms of America's homefront. Since American cities were not being bombed, for example, he showed freedom from fear as children being safely tucked into bed, and freedom from want displayed a traditional holiday dinner, rather than people in Europe or Asia suffering from hunger.

Pearl Harbor

The following telegram reached the White House at 1:40 P.M. on Sunday, December 7, 1941: "AIR RAID PEARL HARBOR—THIS IS NO DRILL." Nearly 400 Japanese warplanes, launched from aircraft carriers that had approached Hawaii without being detected, inflicted heavy damage to the U.S. Pacific fleet. More than 2,400 were killed, 347 airplanes were destroyed, and 14 ships were sunk or severely damaged, including 8 battleships. The fleet's aircraft carriers were away on maneuvers and were spared.

The attack on Pearl Harbor ended all the arguments about neutrality. In addition to the shock of being plunged into the war, Americans found that their sense of fair play had been violated. There had been no declaration of war. In fact, at the time of the attack Japanese diplomats were talking about peace with Secretary of State Cordell Hull. Throughout the war, Americans referred to Pearl Harbor as "the sneak attack." The following selection is an eyewitness account of the attack by a teacher in Honolulu.

FROM

Cornelia MacEwen Hurd's Eyewitness Account

DECEMBER 1941

It was 7:55 A.M. . . . I was sitting on the veranda of our house, about 800 feet above the ocean, and it commanded a view all the way from Diamond Head to Pearl Harbor. I saw the bombs that were dropped in the ocean very, very vividly . . . in fact, I thought it must be the Army Air Force practising. Then I saw that they almost hit the Royal Hawaiian Hotel, and I said to myself, that was awfully close! The splashes were like plumes, going way up in the air. . . .

Then, when I heard over the radio that Hawaii was under attack, I ran to the side of my property . . . and there I saw the most dreadful thing I ever saw in my life. The fire, the blasting of the ships, just one after the other, in flames! I had a good view, and I knew it so well, having been there so many times, the almost enclosed lagoon harbor. And the fire and the blaze and the noise was . . . something I'll never forget. A Japanese plane passed right in front of my yard, not more than forty feet from where I was. It was so vivid I could see the face, the profile, and the rising sun on the plane.

The United States Declares War

The day after the attack on Pearl Harbor, Roosevelt asked Congress to declare war on Japan. Germany and Italy then fulfilled their treaty obligations to Japan by declaring war on the United States. On December 11, Roosevelt returned the favor by asking Congress for a Declaration of War against both countries.

The following is part of Roosevelt's December 8 speech.

FROM

Roosevelt's Address to Congress

DECEMBER 8, 1941

Yesterday, December 7, 1941—a date which will live in infamy—the United States of America was suddenly and deliberately attacked by naval and air forces of the Empire of Japan.

The United States was at peace with that Nation and, at the solicitation of Japan, was still in conversation with its Government and its Emperor looking toward the maintenance of peace in the Pacific. . . .

It will be recorded that the distance of Hawaii from Japan makes it obvious that the attack was deliberately planned many days or even weeks ago. During the intervening time the Japanese Government has deliberately sought to deceive the United States by false statements and expressions of hope for continued peace. . . .

Yesterday the Japanese Government also launched an attack against Malaya.

Last night Japanese forces attacked Hong Kong.

Last night Japanese forces attacked the Philippine Islands.

Last night the Japanese attacked Wake Island.

And this morning the Japanese attacked Midway Island. . . .

No matter how long it may take us to overcome this premeditated invasion, the American people in their righteous might will win through to absolute victory.

I believe that I interpret the will of the Congress and of the people when I assert that we will not only defend ourselves to the uttermost but will make it very certain that this form of treachery shall never again endanger us. . . .

With confidence in our armed forces—and with the unbounding determination of our people—we will gain the inevitable triumph—so help us God.

The Japanese also struck the Philippines, Wake Island, and Midway, as well as the British protectorate of Hong Kong. By the spring of 1942, the Japanese had invaded and conquered the two small U.S. island bases—Guam and Wake Island—and then occupied the Philippines after a series of battles at Bataan and Corregidor against General Douglas MacArthur's combined U.S. and Filipino force.

I ask that the Congress declare that since the unprovoked and dastardly attack by Japan on Sunday, December 7, 1941, a state of war has existed between the United States and the Japanese empire.

War Nerves and Anger

The attack on Pearl Harbor had a remarkable effect—it created a sense of patriotic unity stronger than anything in our history. Within hours of the news, young men were rushing to enlist in the military services and government switchboards were flooded with calls from people who wanted to know what they could do to contribute.

In addition to anger and hatred, especially toward the Japanese, there were fears that our coastal cities were likely to experience the kind of bombing raids the British had been living through. The following selection is a fourteen-year-old boy's account of what life was like for Americans in the months immediately following Pearl Harbor.

The U-Boat Menace

German submarines, moving in groups called "Wolf Packs," caused enormous damage in the early months of the war, sinking almost 700 Allied ships in the Atlantic. The shipping lanes between Atlantic coast ports—Boston, New York, Richmond, Charleston—and South America were hard hit, with 87 ships being sunk off the U.S. coast. Until blackouts were perfected in coastal towns (May 1942), the lights helped the U-boat captains because the Allied ships stood out in silhouette, creating easy targets.

FROM

Howard Still's Letter to His Brother

MARCH 1942

Dear Frank,

It's scary to think of you on a destroyer somewhere in the North Atlantic. Dad said it could be weeks or months before we get a letter from you.

On Sunday, the whole family went to the "Palace" and saw some dumb romantic thing, but the Movietone News [newsreel] was what really hit us. There were a bunch of ships out at sea and lifeboats were pulling sailors out of the water, all the while a freighter was one big ball of flames. Of course everybody thought of you. Mom had to go to the lobby cuz she was crying. Helen [Frank's fiancée] went back to be with her. I'd sure hate to see your ship in a newsreel like that. . . .

Uncle Ralph says it's almost impossible to go onto his town beach now. There is machine guns and sandbags everywhere. Even from the cliff he could see Coast Guard patrols with police dogs, maybe looking for spies or **saboteurs** being put ashore by Nazi subs. He also said he twice saw freighters offshore in flames after being hit by torpedoes. Can you imagine all that going on right where we had that clam bake on Labor Day? I guess wreckage washes ashore a lot.

saboteurs: enemy agents sent to cause destruction.

Relocation of Japanese Americans

Even as Americans were gearing up for a noble patriotic effort, their anger and war jitters led to one serious black mark on their record—the rounding up of all Japanese Americans living on the West Coast and sending them to relocation camps in remote areas of the interior. A total of roughly 110,000 Japanese Americans were sent to these bleak camps, mostly in desert areas of the Rocky Mountain states. Roughly two-thirds of the internees were Nisei—Americans of Japanese ancestry born in the United States; the rest were Isei—born in Japan but legally in the United States as citizens or as resident aliens. No evidence of disloyalty by Japanese Americans was ever found.

The first of the selections that follow is from a government poster announcing the forced evacuation of all Japanese Americans. The second is from the memoirs of Jeanne Wakatsuki, who had been in an internment camp as a child.

A Japanese American relocation camp.

SPECIAL COLLECTIONS DEPT. J. WILLIARD MARRIOT LIBRARY, UNIVERSITY OF UTAH

FROM

A Government Poster

MAY 1942

INSTRUCTIONS TO ALL PERSONS OF
JAPANESE
ANCESTRY

Pursuant to the provisions of Civilian Exclusion Order No. 33, this Headquarters, dated May 3, 1942, all persons of Japanese ancestry, both alien and non-alien, will be evacuated . . . by 12 o'clock noon . . . May 9, 1942.

No Japanese person . . . will be permitted to change residence after 12 o'clock noon . . . Sunday, May 3, 1942, without obtaining special permission from the representative of the Commanding General, Southern California Sector. . . .

The Following Instructions Must Be Observed:

1. A responsible member of each family, preferably the head of the family . . . will report to the Civil Control Station to receive further instructions. . . .

2. Evacuees must carry with them on departure for the Assembly Center, the following property:

   (a) Bedding and linens (no mattress) for each member of the family;

   (b) Toilet articles for each member of the family;

   (c) Extra clothing for each member of the family;

   (d) Sufficient knives, forks, spoons, plates, bowls, and cups for each member of the family;

   (e) Essential personal effects for each member of the family.

All items carried will be securely packaged, tied and plainly marked with the name of the owner and numbered in accordance with instructions obtained at the Civil Control Station. The size and number of packages is limited to that which can be carried by the individual or family group.

Patriotic Citizens

Many internees protested the conditions they were forced to live under and they hated being treated as "the enemy." Their deep faith in America led them to put up with the unfairness and they remained patriotic citizens.

In 1943 the army began recruiting soldiers from the camps. Many served in the tough Italian campaign as the Japanese American 442nd Regimental Combat Team. For its size and length of service, it earned more decorations than any other unit in the nation's history.

FROM

Jeanne Wakatsuki's
Farewell to Manzanar

1 9 7 3

The fact that America had accused us, or excluded us, or imprisoned us, or whatever it might be called, did not change the kind of world we wanted. Most of us were born in this country; we had no other models. Those parks and gardens (built by camp residents) lent it an oriental character, but in most ways it was a totally equipped American small town, complete with schools, churches, Boy Scouts, beauty parlors, neighborhood gossip, fire and police departments, glee clubs, softball leagues, Abbott and Costello movies, tennis courts, and traveling shows. . . .

My sister Lillian was in high school and singing with a hillbilly band called The Sierra Stars—jeans, cowboy hats, two guitars, and a tub bass. And my oldest brother, Bill, led a dance band called The Jive Bombers—brass and rhythm, with cardboard fold-out music stands lettered J.B. Dances were held every weekend in one of the recreation halls. Bill played trumpet and took vocals on Glenn Miller arrangements of such tunes as *In the Mood, String of Pearls,* and

Belated Justice

In 1983, a congressional committee investigated the wartime internment policy and concluded that "race prejudice, war hysteria, and a failure of political leadership" had led to "a grave injustice." The same year, a U.S. District Court overturned a 1944 Supreme Court case justifying internment. In 1988 Congress passed a bill formally apologizing to the nation's Japanese Americans and granted $20,000 to each of the 60,000 survivors for the harm done to them.

Don't Fence Me In. He didn't sing *Don't Fence Me In* out of protest, as if trying quietly to mock the authorities. It just happened to be a hit song one year, and they all wanted to be an up-to-date American swing band. They would blast it out into recreation barracks full of bobby-soxed, jitterbugging couples:

"Oh, give me land, lots of land
Under starry skies above,
Don't fence me in.
Let me ride through the wide
Open country that I love."

Striking Back

In the months after Pearl Harbor, the production of almost all peacetime goods was stopped and U.S. industries rapidly retooled for manufacturing materials for war. Millions of young men volunteered for military service or were drafted, and thousands of women served in auxiliary branches of the services. By the end of the war, roughly fifteen million men and women were in uniform—more than 10 percent of the total population.

Troops, aircraft, ships, and the other materials of war were rushed into action, but, for a few months in 1942, the United States and the Allies suffered more defeats. Very slowly, the American buildup began to make a difference. The Japanese advance in the Pacific was stopped at the naval battles of Coral Sea and Midway in May and June 1942. In the west, American troops arrived in North Africa in time to help the British drive the Germans and Italians off the continent—the first major victory against Hitler's mighty war machine. In late 1942 and 1943, the Russians blunted the German advance against the Soviet Union. At the same time, U.S. and British forces invaded Sicily, then Italy. The fighting in Italy turned into a brutal struggle that lasted almost to the end of the war. The Italians overthrew Mussolini and sued for peace, but the Germans refused to let them stop fighting and sent reinforcements that kept the Allies pinned down in the rugged terrain. In the following selection, a young soldier named Paul Curtis tries to explain to his younger brother what being in war is like.

FROM

A Soldier's Letter from the Italian Front

MAY 1944

Dear Mitchell: Anzio, Italy

As I told you in my last **V-Mail,** I have seen some action—a few hard, hard days in which I saw more than I ever imagined I would. I don't think any man can exactly explain combat. It's beyond words. Take a combination of fear, anger, hunger, thirst, exhaustion, disgust, loneliness, homesickness, and wrap that all up in one reaction and you might approach the feeling. . . . It makes you feel mighty small, helpless, and alone. It's a comfort to know there's one who is present at all times and anywhere ready to help you through. My faith in God has been steadily growing stronger all along. Without faith, I don't see how anyone could stand this. It all seems so useless, but I realize Germany must be stopped. . . .

I thought I had been tired before in my life, but nothing like this; but still you can and do go on. Every time you stop you dig a hole, which has saved many lives. The ground is so hard and dry that digging is very hard. You don't get so very hungry, but thirst drives you crazy. I have drunk water with everything in it and liked it. You have no energy but still you go on.

The battle seems like something in a faraway land, and everything seems sad, lonely, and dark. The roar is even as bad as the movies have it. The cries of the wounded are pitiful. They seem so helpless. . . . You wanted to know how I felt after I saw action and I have told you all I can that will pass the censors; I imagine all new men feel about the same and I know old men feel differently and so will I, but that's for now.

V-mail: lightweight airmail letter forms.

Air Power

Aircraft—both bombers and small, speedy fighters—played a crucial role throughout the war. Hitler had counted on air power to pave the way for his invasion of England, but the stubborn resistance of British aviators forced him to cancel invasion plans. The Allies had no way to strike directly at Germany except through air power until late in 1944. The British flew nighttime raids over German cities, industries, and ports, while Americans flew the more dangerous daylight raids. These bombing runs hurt Germany's war production and eroded Hitler's airforce, the Luftwaffe. But the cost was enormous. By 1944, the Germans had shot down 18,500 U.S. aircraft and more than 60,000 airmen. In the next reading, an American flyer describes a dangerous raid on Nazi oil refineries in Ploesti, Romania, the source of half of Germany's petroleum. The attack, in August 1943, cost the lives of nearly 25 percent of the men in the 178 B-24 bombers.

Submarines: The "Silent Service"

The submarines were called the "Silent Service" because their success depended on absolute silence. In the Pacific war against Japan, the U.S. submarines were a main ingredient in turning back the Japanese military. In the beginning, the U.S. torpedoes were poorly made and rarely hit their targets. But, by mid-1943, the problems were solved and in that year alone the U.S. subs sank 22 enemy warships and 296 merchant ships. The Silent Service sank more Japanese ships than either U.S. warships or aircraft.

FROM

A Bomber Pilot's Letter Home

AUGUST 1943

Dear Mom & Dad & All:

. . . Went on the raid in the heart of Romania. Just northwest of Bucharest at the city of Ploesti. . . . Before we came to our turning point into the target which was the Vega-Romano Refinery our left waist gunner was killed by machine gun fire. I asked Major Dessert to take over as co-pilot and I went back and took the waist gun. We were down to 50 or 60 feet above the ground and were just coming over a village before Ploesti. The people in their very pretty native costumes (the day being Sunday) were waving and standing in the streets.

Just after we passed over that village I saw an 88mm **flak** battery consisting of 4 guns. They were pointed at us. Four

flak: antiaircraft.

Germans or Romanians were handling shells . . . and I opened fire on them. Killed all four of them and blew up something in the battery. Those 4 guns did not fire anymore.

We then were coming into the edge of Ploesti and I saw a 6-gun battery and another of 8 guns. I shot approximately 150 rounds into each battery and completely wiped both out. But not before they got one of our wing men. . . .

Then into town I go and on every house top and building there were guns. I fired constantly. . . . I hear our bombardier say there is the target at 12 O'clock. Then another one of our planes go down. That was Nick Stompolis of Kalamazoo, Michigan. His co-pilot is Ivan Canfield of San Antonio, my very best friend in the 409th. From their bomb bay doors on back he's in flames. He is trying to hold the ship in the air till he gets over the town but can't make it. So seeing that he can't he turns for the biggest building in town and goes head on to make it quick. Which in my estimation was the most heroic move on the raid. . . .

Then there is the target with oil storage tanks blowing up all around us. . . . and I see a Liberator (bomber) with its wheels down . . . and he lands in a field and the last thing I saw was 6 guys running like mad to escape capture and try to get to . . . Yugoslavia and join the Guerilla Bands. . . . Dad if you get a chance go to Caldwell and see Mr. H. H. Womble and tell him his son [the pilot of the Liberator] is pretty positively alive and either a prisoner of war or a guerilla warrior now in Yugoslavia. . . . Well . . . we turned for home and made it back okay. The mission was 13 hours long and a little over 2400 miles. The 409th is only a shadow of its former self.

Commander David McCampbell, World War II navy ace.

Homefront Warriors

President Roosevelt called on the nation to become the "arsenal of democracy"—to produce the war materials and food that would be needed by the United States, and by the Allies, to defeat the Axis powers. The American people accepted the challenge with extraordinary energy and dedication. Within weeks of Pearl Harbor, practically all peacetime production had stopped and some 200,000 businesses made the transition to manufacturing war materials. By 1943, American factories were outproducing the industries of Germany, Japan, and Italy combined.

The vast majority of Americans were involved in the war effort. Fifteen million served in the armed forces, an incredible number that translated into one out of every ten Americans being in uniform. By January 1942, nearly six million men and women were enrolled in civil defense programs, including 700,000 air raid wardens who patrolled the streets during blackouts to make sure all lights were out. Another 600,000 served in the Ground Observation Corps, manning observation posts to scan the skies for enemy aircraft. People were also involved in less formal ways, for example, by working in defense plants and shipyards, buying War Bonds, collecting scrap material for recycling, and planting "Victory" Gardens to raise their own table vegetables. In addition, every man, woman, and child received a ration book, with coupons for the purchase of major food items as well as shoes and gasoline. The ration system helped to guarantee that the armed forces had ample food and that the civilian population shared shortages in a way that was fair.

FROM

Roosevelt's Fireside Chat

APRIL 1942

We are now in this war. We are all in it—all the way. Every single man, woman, and child is a partner in the most tremendous undertaking of our American history. . . .

It will not only be a long war, it will be a hard war. The

United States does not consider it a sacrifice to do all one can, to give one's best to our Nation, when the Nation is fighting for its existence and its future life. . . .

There is one front and one battle where everyone in the United States—every man, woman, and child—is in action, and will be privileged to remain in action throughout this war. That front is right here at home, in our daily lives, and in our daily tasks. Here at home everyone will have the privilege of making whatever self-denial is necessary, not only to supply our fighting men, but to keep the economic structure of our country fortified and secure during the war and after the war.

Kids Do Their Part

With kids leading the way as the most avid scrap collectors, every household was transformed into a recycling center. Even cooking fats were carefully preserved to convert into glycerine for explosives. People found a special appeal in reading frequent news items on scrap conversions, like a single tire having enough rubber for 12 gas masks, or an old shovel containing enough iron for 4 hand grenades, and a radiator being equal to 17 rifles.

But children were not just eager scrap collectors. In mid-1943, the government relaxed child-labor laws, which enabled three million kids, ages 12 to 17, to work in defense plants. Young people were also energetic buyers of War Stamps and War Bonds. In 1944, school sales of stamps and bonds provided the funds for 2,900 planes, 11,700 parachutes, and 44,000 jeeps.

Women Workers

Roughly ten million women were in the work force before Pearl Harbor, and the number increased to eighteen million during the war. There were still strong feelings, shared by women as well as men, that a woman's place was in the home, and most of the wartime workers were laid off as soon as the war ended. In the following reading, Sybil Lewis, an African American, tells of the prejudice she encountered as a black and as a woman.

FROM

A Woman War Worker's Recollections

1942–1945

I saw an ad in the newspaper offering to train women for defense work. I went . . . and applied. . . . After two tries, they accepted me . . . and taught me how to rivet. Then they put me to work in the plant riveting small airplane parts, mainly gasoline tanks.

The women worked in pairs. I was the riveter, and this big strong white girl from a cotton farm in Arkansas worked as the bucker. The riveter used a gun to shoot rivets through the metal and fasten it together. The bucker used a bucking bar on the other side of the metal to smooth out the rivets. Bucking . . required more muscle. Riveting required more skill.

One day the boss came around and said, "We've decided to make some changes." He assigned the white girl to do the riveting and me to do the bucking. I wanted to know why. He said, "Well, we just interchange once in a while." But I was never given the riveting

Norman Rockwell's famous Rosie the Riveter, wearing the required bandana, was modeled after a real woman, Rose Monroe, who worked in an aircraft plant in Michigan.

COURTESY OF THE NORMAN ROCKWELL MUSEUM AT STOCKBRIDGE, MASSACHUSETTS

job back. That was the first encounter I had with segregation in California, and it didn't sit too well with me. . . .

[In 1943] I passed a training course in welding and they employed me at the shipyards. . . . There I ran into another kind of discrimination: because I was a woman, I was paid less than a man for doing the same job. . . . Once the foreman told me I had to go on the skids—the long docks alongside the hull. I said, "That sounds pretty dangerous. Will I make more than one-twenty an hour?" And he said, "No, one-twenty is the top pay you'll get." But we both knew the men got more.

D-Day: The Allied Invasion of Normandy

By 1944 the Allies were ready to strike at the heart of the German and Japanese empires. In the Pacific, American and Allied forces started an "island-hopping" campaign—invading major islands held by the Japanese, but bypassing others, with the U.S. Navy preventing those islands from being evacuated or reinforced. The grim jungle warfare continued through 1944 and half of 1945.

In the West, England had been turned into a base for the largest invasion force in history—crossing the English Channel to strike at the Normandy coast of France. The invasion of Normandy, code-named D-Day, consisted of 175,000 assault troops, 5,000 ships and landing craft, and 11,000 aircraft. German defenders had built massive defenses along the coast, but they didn't know precisely where or when the Allies would land. Supreme Allied Commander Dwight D. Eisenhower was keenly aware that there were only a few days each month when the tides would be right for the invasion, but fierce storms sweeping in off the North Sea canceled one possible day after another. Finally, when told there would be a brief break in the storms, "Ike" gave the signal.

The following readings provide a glimpse of these crucial hours. In the first reading, the soldiers' favorite reporter, Ernie Pyle, who landed after the first waves of troops, describes the German defenses; in the second, a Brooklyn G.I. describes his part in the historic invasion.

FROM

An Article by Ernie Pyle

JUNE 1944

In this column I want to tell you what the opening of the second front in this one sector entailed, so that you can know and appreciate and forever be humbly grateful to those both dead and alive who did it for you.

Ashore, facing us, were more enemy troops than we had in our assault waves. The advantages were all theirs; the disadvantages all ours. The Germans were dug into positions that they had been working on for months. . . . A 100-foot bluff a couple hundred yards back from the beach had great concrete gun emplacements built right into the hilltop. These opened to the sides instead of to the front, thus making it very hard for naval fire from the sea to reach them. They could shoot parallel with the beach and cover every foot of it for miles with artillery fire. . . .

Our only exits from the beach were several swales or valleys, each about 100 yards wide. The Germans made the most of these funnel-shaped traps, sowing them with buried mines. They contained, also, barbed-wire entanglements with mines attached, and machine guns firing from the slopes.

This is what was on the shore. But our men had to go through a maze nearly as deadly as this before they even got ashore. . . . And yet we got on.

U.S. troops hit the beach on D-Day, June 6, 1944.

FROM

A Private's Letter to His Wife

JUNE 1944

In the far away distance I could hear the rumble of the artillery and the brrrp-brrrp of machine gun fire.

The elements were at their worst and our landing craft was half filled with water. We used our helmuts to throw it overboard and I never thought we would make it. Some of the boats never reached shore. It was a horrible sight.

Finally the word came—Let's go—and there we were in combat, something new in my life. But oh, what an experience.

We didn't have a chance to fight back, as we were dropped in water over our heads. No one's fault as the entire beach was strewn with mines. With a stream of lead coming towards us, we were at the mercy of the Germans and we had all to do to reach shore and recuperate. I floated around in water for about one hour and was more dead than alive. Tried to land at several places, but always had to withdraw. It was impossible to get ashore.

. . . Got to the beach half frozen and almost unable to move and then I passed out. How long I remained there, I don't recall, but when I came to, the fighting was at a climax. Pulled myself together and sought a rifle and around I went trying to locate my outfit. It didn't take long to spot them and was I glad. But gracious Lord, what was left of them, just a handful, about 25 out of 160. The battalion was almost wiped out, 800 casualties out of 1000 men.

Our position was desperate, but with sheer will, fear and luck we overcame all obstacles and pushed inland to capture Vierville-sur-Mer, our first town. The price was high but covered ourselves with glory and for that we received the Presidential Citation.

In the hours before the invasion, Allied ships and bombers had shelled the defenses for hours and, before dawn, British and U.S. paratroopers and glider units landed behind the lines to disrupt enemy communications. While some of the landings encountered light opposition, the Americans at the beach code-named Omaha became so bogged down that the commander almost withdrew them. But the GIs pushed through and took the beach, although they suffered one-third of the day's casualties.

The Shock of Hitler's Death Camps

After Normandy, the Allies pushed inland rapidly, while the Russians advanced from the east, squeezing Hitler's fortress into an ever-smaller area. First the Russians, in late 1944, and then the Americans and British a few weeks later, faced the horror of Hitler's death camps—Aushwitz, Buchenwald, Bergen-Belsen, Dachau, and a dozen others. There had been rumors for two years or more that the Nazis were trying to destroy Europe's Jews as well as other "undesirables," including Catholics, the disabled, Gypsies, and homosexuals, by systematically sending them to these camps for extermination. An estimated twelve million people died in the camps, half of them Jews. President Eisenhower was so horrified that he quickly assembled scores of journalists and photographers to record these crimes. The horror of the Holocaust, and the discovery of it, took a good deal of the luster off the Allied victory. In the following selection, Staff Sergeant Horace Evers wrote to his parents about Dachau.

FROM

Sergeant Evers's Letter Home

MAY 1945

I had the misfortune of seeing DACHAU yesterday and I still find it hard to believe what my eyes told me.—

A railroad runs alongside the camp and as we walked toward the box cars on the track I thought of some of the stories I previously had read about DACHAU and was glad of the chance to see for myself just to prove once and for all that what I had heard was propaganda.—But *no* it wasn't propaganda at all—if anything some of the truth had been held back. . . . I have seen a lot of death . . . but nothing has ever stirred me as much as this. I can't shrug off the feeling of utter hate I now hold for these [German] people. . . .

The first box car I came to had about 30 what were once humans in it.—All were just bone with a layer of skin over them. Most of the eyes were open and had an indescribable look about them. They had that beaten "what did I do to deserve this" look. Twenty to thirty other box cars were the same. Bodies on top of each other—no telling how many. No identification as far as I could see.—And then into the camp itself.—Filthy barracks suitable for about 200 persons held 1500. 160,000 persons were originally in the camp and 32,000 were alive (or almost alive) when we arrived.

The Death of Roosevelt

Another event that dimmed the glory of Germany's surrender in May 1945 was the death of President Roosevelt on April 12. FDR had been elected to a third presidential term in 1940, breaking the two-term tradition established by George Washington. He won a fourth term in 1944 in the midst of the war, making Missouri senator Harry S. Truman his vice president. The strain of twelve years in office was too much for Roosevelt and he died only a few weeks after his fourth inauguration. He was sixty-three years old.

The Americans and the Russians Meet

The Soviet Union had maintained an uneasy alliance with the United States and the other Western allies, but neither side really trusted the other. Joseph Stalin, the iron-fisted dictator of the world's only Communist nation (at that time), was eager to push Soviet interests into the portions of Eastern Europe that were being liberated from German occupation by Soviet troops. British prime minister Winston Churchill felt that the Allies should do all in their power to prevent any expansion of Soviet power, but President Roosevelt and his staff were hopeful that the wartime alliance would hold together. The Americans also felt that the major objective was the destruction of Hitler's empire.

American and Russian troops met at the Elbe River on April 25, 1945, just before the Soviets and the Western Allies crushed the remnants of Nazi Germany between them. An American private with a keen sense of

The Coming of the Cold War

In the heady days of Germany's surrender in May 1945, very few Americans were worried about the Soviet Union or the possibility of Communist expansion. Only gradually over the next two years did people come to see that the United States was in the grip of a new kind of war, a Cold War, with the Communist Soviet Union as the major adversary.

history, Joseph Polowsky, described the meeting in an interview with the journalist Studs Terkel.

FROM

A Soldier's Account of the American-Soviet Meeting

APRIL 1945

A phone call comes in from battalion headquarters. They want a patrol to be formed immediately, seven jeeps, twenty-eight men, to go about five miles in front of the lines to see if they could get some sign of the Russians. . . . Of course, we were saddened to learn that President Roosevelt had died about two weeks earlier. We also knew that the United Nations was being born in San Francisco on the very same day, 25th of April. Can you imagine? The very day we linked up with the Russians at the Elbe River. . . .

It was a tremendous feeling to see the Elbe. This was about 11:30 in the morning. The Elbe is a swift-running river about 175 yards wide. Kotzebue [the U.S. platoon leader] shot up two green flares. After about ten minutes . . . the Russians waved at us and gave the signal to approach their lines.

Kotzebue, who is a very religious man, was much moved. He couldn't talk Russian. The Russians couldn't talk English. He said, "Joe, let's make a resolution with these Russians . . . this would be an important day in the lives of the two countries and the symbolism of all the civilian dead. Talk to them in German." As I was translating to Kotzebue in English, one of the Russians who knew German was translating to the other Russians. It was very informal, but it was a solemn moment. There were tears in the eyes of most of us. Perhaps a sense of foreboding that things might not be as perfect in the future as we anticipated. We embraced. We swore never to forget.

Winning the War in the Pacific

In the Pacific, the Japanese had turned each of their captured islands into an armed fortress, manned by troops who rarely surrendered. The first island the Allies fought to reclaim was Guadalcanal, landing 11,000 marines in August 1942. Even with heavy army reinforcements, the brutal jungle warfare continued until the following February. This costly experience taught the Allied leaders the importance of an island-hopping strategy.

Each island conquest took the Allies closer to the main Japanese islands. After a long, bitter struggle to retake the Philippines, the Allies next invaded the tiny island of Iwo Jima, 8 square miles of rock defended by 21,000 Japanese who would not surrender. The weeks of fighting, with nearly 7,000 marines killed, was one factor in the Allied decision to use the world's first atomic bombs on Hiroshima and Nagasaki in Japan, killing about 100,000 people outright, while thousands more died from the effects of radiation. President Truman, with the support of the Allies, made the decision to use the bombs because it was expected that an invasion of Japan itself could cost up to one million American lives.

In the first of the following readings, marine Ted Allenby tells how his experience on Iwo Jima influenced his thinking about the atomic bomb. The second selection is by Philip Morrison, one of the physicists who helped develop the bomb in a secret project code-named "Manhattan."

FROM

Ted Allenby's Account of Iwo Jima

1945

The men who landed . . . on February 19, 1945—well, there aren't many of them left. The casualty rate was enormous. It was ghastly. Iwo was a volcanic island with very little concealment. . . . It was almost like a piece of the moon that had dropped down to earth. . . .

Navajo "Code Talkers"

Secret codes were vital to both sides throughout the war. When the Japanese broke the American code, a foolproof substitute was needed. The solution was provided by thirty marines who were Navajos. Simply talking in their own language over the two-way radios then in use constituted a code that the Japanese were never able to break.

[After Iwo Jima, we] were . . . planning for the landing on the Japanese mainland. . . . Our intelligence people [later] told us we would have landed at Chigasaki. Later, when I was in Japan as a Navy chaplain . . . I got off the train at Chigasaki and walked down to the beach where we would have landed. I got a chill. It was Iwo Jima magnified a hundred times. . . . They would have wiped us out.

Right now, I'm totally against war in any form. I say yes, that bomb was a ghastly thing. I was in Hiroshima and I stood at ground zero. I saw deformities that I had never seen before. . . . But I also know that had we landed in Japan, we would have faced greater carnage than Normandy. It would probably have been the most bloody invasion in history. . . .

The only way we took Iwo Jima was because we outnumbered them three to one. Still they held us at bay as long as they did. We'd had to starve them out, month after month after month. As it was, they were really down to eating grass and bark off trees. So I feel split about Hiroshima. The damn thing probably saved my life.

Okinawa and the Kamikaze Attacks

The invasion of Okinawa, after Iwo Jima, was another bitter fight that helped convince President Truman to use the atomic bomb. More than 7,000 Americans died taking the island. Of the 120,000 Japanese defenders, 100,000 died rather than surrender.

Okinawa was also the scene of Japanese suicide planes—2,000 pilots who became "kamikaze" and dove their planes into American ships. In their first assault, 355 planes were involved in an attack called kikisui ("floating chrysanthemums"), where the pilots crashed into ships off the Okinawa coast. Over the two months of the attacks, the kamikazes sank 29 U.S. ships, damaged 368 others, and killed an estimated 5,000 Americans.

FROM

A Physicist's Recollections of the Manhattan Project

1945

The test [code-named Trinity] was set for Monday morning. I went down the Thursday before, guarded in a convoy of automobiles, carrying the core, the little ball of plutonium. I designed the ball. We assembled the bomb in the high explosive only for the second time. We were all afraid. . . .

From ten miles away we saw the unbelievably brilliant flash. . . . [Following the successful test] I was sent to Wendover Air Force Base at Wendover, Utah. . . . I loaded the plane called *Bock's Car* . . . named after Captain Bock . . . and somebody else loaded the *Enola Gay*. The takeoff was dangerous, because there was no way of rendering it safe. . . . *Bock's Car*'s bomb fell on Nagasaki three days after *Enola Gay*'s fell on Hiroshima.

We heard the news of Hiroshima from the airplane itself, a coded message . . . then the people came back with photographs. I remember looking at them with awe and terror. We knew a terrible thing had been unleashed. The men had a great party that night to celebrate, but we didn't go. Almost no physicists went to it. We obviously killed a hundred thousand people and that was nothing to have a party about. . . .

I was of the opinion that a warning to the Japanese might work. I was disappointed when the military said you don't warn.

Realize this: the Air Force had bombed sixty-six Japanese cities and towns before the end of the war. Ninety-nine big air raids and sixty-six targets. The place was destroyed. From our point of view, the atomic bomb was not a discontinuity. We were just carrying on more of the same, only it was much cheaper. For that war, it was just one more city destroyed. We had already destroyed sixty-six; what's two more?

War Casualties

Large areas of the world, especially Europe and eastern Asia, suffered tremendous damage in the war. The total death toll has been estimated at fifty million, including the twelve million lives destroyed in Hitler's death camps. Millions of refugees wandered through Europe with no homes or families to return to.

In comparison, the United States suffered light losses. There were no bombing raids on U.S. soil. The economies of the warring nations were in shambles, while U.S. industrial and agricultural output had never been higher. The country suffered 400,000 war dead, a number that seems small compared to the Soviet Union, where roughly 10 percent of the population died. However, in addition to the Americans killed, wounded, or listed as missing, almost every American family lived for three years with the constant fear of receiving a government telegram saying, "We regret to inform you. . . ."

V-J Day

When Germany surrendered in May 1945, Americans celebrated V-E Day—victory in Europe. People felt a great sense of relief after the years of sacrifice and loss, but the joy was tempered by the knowledge that the war against Japan continued. The death of Roosevelt and the discovery of the Holocaust also dampened the enthusiasm.

V-J Day—Victory over Japan—was different.

Alfred Eisenstaedt's memorable V-J Day photo at New York's Times Square

FROM

"Japan Surrenders: End of War,"
New York Times

AUGUST 15, 1945

Five days of waiting . . . came to an end a moment or two after seven o'clock last night. And the metropolis exploded its emotions . . . with atomic force.

"Official—Truman announces Japanese surrender."

Those were the magic words flashed on the moving electric sign of the Times Tower . . . that touched off an unparalleled demonstration in Times Square, packed with half a million persons.

The victory roar that greeted the announcement beat upon the eardrums until it numbed the senses. For twenty minutes wave after wave of that joyous roar surged forth.

Restraint was thrown to the winds. Those in the crowds in the streets tossed hats, boxes, and flags into the air. From those leaning perilously out of the windows of office buildings and hotels came a shower of paper, confetti, streamers. Men and women embraced—there were no strangers in New York yesterday. Some were hilarious, others cried softly.

By 7:30 P.M. the crowd in the Square had risen to 750,000 persons; by 8:45 it had swelled to 800,000 and the number continued to rise. . . . Individual movement was virtually impossible; one moved not in the crowd but with it.

SOURCES

PART I: A Nation in Transition

Atlantic Monthly, July 1876: from William Dean Howells, "A Sennight of the Centennial," in Lally Weymouth, *America in 1876: The Way We Were* (New York: Random House, 1976), pp. 27–28.

"The Tele-phone," *New York Tribune,* November 4, 1876: from David C. King, *The Age of Technology: 19th-Century American Inventors* (Carlisle, Mass.: Discovery Enterprises, 1997), pp. 35–36.

F. C. Beach, *Scientific American,* December 1877: from David C. King, *Thomas Alva Edison: The King of Inventors* (Carlisle, Mass.: Discovery Enterprises, 1995), p. 29.

New York Times, September 5, 1882: from *Liberty and Union* (Boston: Houghton Mifflin, 1973), vol. 2, pp. 49–50.

Hamlin Garland, *A Son of the Middle Border,* F. P. Collier & Son, 1914, 1917; reprinted by Macmillan Company, p. 211: excerpted in David C. King, et al., *The United States and Its People* (Menlo Park, Calif.: Addison Wesley Publishing Co., 1996), p. 397.

Edward Corsi, *In the Shadow of Liberty* (New York: Macmillan Company, 1935), pp. 3–4.

A Letter from the Chicago World's Fair, from Arthur Meadows, ed., *The Chicago World's Fair: Reports of Visitors,* Chicago 1893; excerpts in King, et al., *The United States and Its People,* p. 896.

Andrew Carnegie, *Gospel of Wealth,* New York, 1900: from Henry Steele Commager and Allan Nevins, *The Heritage of America* (Boston: Little, Brown, 1939), pp. 951–953.

Mary Antin, *The Promised Land,* 1912: from ibid., pp. 880–884.

Giuseppe Giacosa, *Impressions of America,* 1908: adapted from *The Annals of America,* vol. 13, 1905–1915, *The Progressive Era* (Chicago: Encyclopedia Britannica, 1969), pp. 121–123.

A Statement by John D. Rockefeller Jr., 1903: from William H. Ghent, *Our Benevolent Feudalism,* 1903; excerpts in Marion Brady and Howard Brady, *Idea and Action in American History* (Englewood Cliffs, N.J.: Prentice-Hall, 1977), p. 316.

Andrew Carnegie, "Wealth," 1889: from the *North American Review,* vol. 148, 1889; excerpts in ibid., p. 314.

George Rice's Testimony, 1889: from Brady and Brady, *Idea and Action,* p. 315.

John Spargo, *The Bitter Cry of the Children,* 1906 (New York: Macmillan Company, 1906), pp. 159–160.

Samuel Gompers's Autobiography, 1877: from Gompers, *Seventy Years of Life and Labor* (New York: E.P. Dutton and Co., 1925), pp.181–182.

PART II: Expansion and Reform

Charles J. Post's Memoirs, 1900: from Post, *The Little War of Private Post* (Boston: Little, Brown & Co., 1960); excerpts in Bernard A. Weisberger, *Life History of the United States,* vol. 8, *Reaching for Empire* (New York: Time, 1964), pp. 140–141.

President McKinley's Recollections, 1900: from Charles S. Olcott, *The Life of William McKinley,* vol. 2 (Boston: Houghton Mifflin Co., 1916), pp. 109–111.

A Speech by Senator George Hoar, *Congressional Record,* 55th Cong., 3d sess., pp. 493–503, quoted in *The Annals of America,* vol. 12, 1895–1904, *Populism, Imperialism, and Reform,* p. 252.

Jane Addams, "Hull House, Chicago: An Effort toward Social Democracy," 1893: from *Forum* 14 (1892–1893), pp. 226–227; excerpts in Robert C. Cotner, *Readings in American History,* vol. 2, *1865 to the Present* (Boston: Houghton Mifflin, 1976), pp. 132f.

Frances Perkins's Account of the Triangle Shirtwaist Factory Fire, 1911: from King et al., *The United States and Its People,* p. 441.

"T.R.'s Road to the White House," 1902: from *New York Sun,* March 12, 1902; excerpts in Martin Ridge et al., *Liberty and Union,* vol. 2 (Boston: Houghton Mifflin, 1973), p. 212.

Mark Sullivan, *Our Times: America at the Birth of the 20th Century,* 1926 (New York: Charles Scribner's Sons, 1926; renewed, 1996), pp. 247–248.

Theodore Roosevelt, *The New Nationalism,* 1910: adapted from Brady and Brady, *Idea and Action,* pp.350–351.

Upton Sinclair, *The Jungle,* 1906: from *Annals of America,* vol. 13, *The Progressive Era,* Chicago: Encyclopedia Britannica, 1969), pp. 74–75.

From *Original Rights* by Ida B. Wells, 1910: adapted from Ida B. Wells, "How Enfranchisement Stops Lynching," *Original Rights* magazine, June 1910; excerpts in Milton Melzer, ed., *In Their Own Words: A History of the American Negro,* vol. 2, *1865–1916* (New York: Thomas Y. Crowell, 1965), pp. 154–161.

Outlook Magazine, June 1915: adapted from Editors of Time-Life Books, *Our American Century: End of Innocence, 1910–1926* (Alexandria, Va.: Time-Life Books, 1998), p. 49.

PART III: America in the First World War

The "Zimmermann Note," March 1917: from Ridge et al., *Liberty and Union,* vol. 2, p. 226.

President Wilson, War Message to Congress, April 2, 1917: from Samuel Eliot Morrison, The *Oxford History of the American People* (New York: Oxford University Press, 1965), pp. 859–860.

"The First Lady Marine," 1917: from Kempler F. Crowling, ed., *Dear Folks at Home* (Boston: Houghton Mifflin, 1919), p. 16.

Buffalo Courier, July 1918: from Sellers, Charles G. et al., *As It Happened: A History of the United States* (New York: McGraw-Hill, 1975), p. 312.

"Over There," 1917: by George M. Cohan, in *Annals of America,* vol. 14, *World War and Prosperity, 1916–1929,* p. 117.

General Pershing's Cable to Washington, June 1918: from Andrew Carroll, ed., *War Letters: Extraordinary Correspondence from American Wars* (New York: Washington Square Press, 2002), pp. 139–140.

An Anonymous Soldier's Account, 1917: From Sullivan, *Our Times,* vol. 5, p. 29.

The Diary of Norman Roberts, 1918: from William Matthews and Dixon Wecter, eds., *Our Soldiers Speak, 1775–1918* (Boston: Little, Brown & Co., 1943), pp. 302–304.

Lieutenant Ed Lukert's Letter to His Wife, June 1918: from Carroll, *War Letters,* p. 157.

Quentin Roosevelt's Letter Home, July 1918: from ibid., p.145.

Corporal Elmer W. Sherwood's Diary, October 30, 1918: from Josef and Dorothy Berger, eds., *Diary of America* (New York: Simon and Schuster, 1957), pp. 541–542.

Speech by President Woodrow Wilson, 1919: from Rebecca Brooks Gruver, *An American History,* vol. 2 (Reading, Mass.: Addison-Wesley, 1981), p. 645.

Speech by Henry Cabot Lodge, 1919: from ibid., p. 645.

PART IV: The "Roaring Twenties"

Henry Ford, *My Life and Work* (New York: Doubleday, Page and Co., 1922), pp. 79–82.

"The Road to Freedom," *Motor Car,* 1922: from Sullivan, *Our Times,* vol. 4, p. 373.

Lloyd Lewis, "The Deluxe Picture Palace," *New Republic,* March 27, 1929: from George E. Mowry, ed., *The Twenties: Fords, Flappers and Fanatics* (Englewood Cliffs, N.J.: Prentice-Hall, 1965), pp. 57–59.

"67,000 See Illinois Beat Michigan," *New York Times,* September 20, 1924: excerpt in ibid., p. 83.

"Yanks Rout Pirates," *New York Times,* September 8, 1927: excerpt in ibid., p. 86.

W. O. McGeehan, "Our Trudy," 1926: quoted in *This Fabulous Century,* vol. 3, *1920–1930* (New York: Time-Life Books, 1969), p. 136.

Frederick Lewis Allen, *Only Yesterday,* 1931: from Frederick Lewis Allen, *Only Yesterday* (New York: Harper and Row, 1931), p. 231.

Preston Slosson, *The Great Crusade and After, 1914–1928* (New York: Macmillan Co., 1930, 1958), pp. 151–157.

Felix von Luckner, "Prohibition in America," 1926: from *Annals of America,* vol. 14, *1916–1928, World War and Prosperity,* p. 584.

Hiram W. Evans, "The Klan's Fight for Americanism," 1926: from *North American Review,* March–April–May, 1926, p. 33; reprinted in Mowry, *The Twenties,* pp. 137–139.

"'Leven-cent Cotton," c. 1925: adapted from Bob Miller and Emma Dermer in Joe Glazer, ed., Songs of Work and Freedom (New York: 1960); reprinted in *Annals of America,* vol. 14, p. 573.

James A. Rogers, "Jazz at Home," 1925: from *Survey,* March, 1925; reprinted in *Annals,* ibid., p. 665–667.

Langston Hughes, "Lament for Dark Peoples," 1926: from Langston Hughes, *Weary Blues* (New York: Alfred A. Knopf, 1926), p. 101.

"The Child Stylelites of Baltimore," 1929: from *The New Republic,* August 28, 1929, p. 37; reprinted in Mowry, *The Twenties,* p. 73.

PART V: The Great Depression and the New Deal

Jonathan Norton Leonard, Eyewitness Report, October 1929: Jonathan Norton Leonard, *Three Years Down* (New York: J.B. Lippinoctt Co., 1944), pp. 80–82.

The Journal of E.W. Bakke, April 1933: from E. W. Bakke, *The Unemployed Worker* (New Haven: Yale University. Press, 1940), pp. 171–172.

Charles R. Walker, "Relief and Revolution," 1932: from *Forum* 88 (1932) pp. 73–74, in Janet Beyer and JoAnne B. Weisman, *The Great Depression* (Carlisle, Mass.: Discovery Enterprises, 1995), p. 16.

Roosevelt, Inaugural Address, March 4, 1933: from Roger Butterfield, *The American Past* (New York: Simon and Schuster, 1957), p. 416.

Frances Perkins, Memoirs, 1946: Adapted from Frances Perkins, *The Roosevelt I Knew* (New York: Viking Press, 1946), pp. 166–173.

Luther Wandall, "A Negro in the CCC," 1935: from *The Crisis,* vol. 42, August 1935; excerpts in King, *Readings,* p. 100.

Lorena Hickok, Letter to Eleanor Roosevelt, November 1933: from Richard Lowitt and Maurine Beasley, eds., *One Third of a Nation: Lorena Hickok Reports on the Great Depression* (Urbana: University of Illinois Press, 1981), pp. 91–92.

John Steinbeck, *The Grapes of Wrath,* 1939 (New York: Viking Press, 1957).

Dust Bowl Humor from James D. Horan, *The Desperate Years* (New York: Bonanza Books, 1962), p. 165.

Eleanor Roosevelt, *On My Own,* 1958: excerpts in Gruver, *An American History,* vol. 2, p. 704.

Woody Guthrie, "So Long (It's Been Good to Know Yuh)," c. 1937: adapted from Glazer, ed., *Songs of Work and Freedom.*

PART VI: The Second World War

Edward R. Murrow, Radio Broadcast, October 10, 1940: from C. L. Sulzberger and editors of American Heritage, *The American Heritage History of World War II* (New York: American Heritage Publishing/Bonanza Books, 1966), p. 114–115.

Charles A. Lindbergh, Speech to the America First Committee, May 1941: from Cotner, *Readings in American History,* vol. 2, pp. 277–278.

Cornelia MacEwen Hurd's Eyewitness Account, December, 1941: from Roy Hooper, ed., *Americans Remember the Homefront: An Oral Narrative* (New York: Hawthorne Books, 1977); excerpts in Linda R. Monk, ed., *Ordinary*

Americans (Alexandria, Va.: Close Up Foundation, 1994), p. 191.

Roosevelt's Address to Congress, December 8, 1941: from Samuel I. Rosenman, *1941: The Call to Battle Stations* (New York: Harper and Brothers, 1950), p. 514.

Howard Still's Letter to His Brother, March 1942: adapted from Ridge, *Liberty and Union,* vol. 2, p. 292.

Government Poster, May 1942: from Takeo Kaneshiro, ed., *Internees: War Relocation Center Memoirs and Diaries* (New York: Vantage Press, 1976), p. 27.

Jeanne Wakatsuki and James D. Houston, *Farewell to Manzanar* (Boston: Houghton Mifflin, 1973), p. 280.

A Soldier's Letter from the Italian Front, May 1944: from Carroll, *War Letters,* p. 233.

A Bomber Pilot's Letter Home, August 1943: from ibid., pp. 201–202.

Roosevelt's Fireside Chat, December 9, 1941: from Rosenman, p. 522.

A Woman War Worker's Recollections, 1942–45: from Mark Jonathan Harris, Franklin D. Mitchell, and Steven J. Schechter, *The Homefront: America During World War II* (New York: G.P. Putnam's Sons, 1984), p. 328.

Article by Ernie Pyle, June 1944: from David Nichols, ed., *The Best of Ernie Pyle* (New York: Simon and Schuster, 1986), pp. 214–215.

A Private's Letter to His Wife, June 1944: from Carroll, *War Letters,* p. 245.

Sergeant Evers's Letter Home, May 1945: from ibid., p. 275.

A Soldier's Account of the American-Soviet Meeting, April 1945: from Studs Terkel, *The Good War: An Oral History of World War II* (New York: Ballantine Books, 1984), pp. 444–448.

Ted Allenby's Account of Iwo Jima, 1945: from Linda Monk, ed., *Ordinary Americans: U.S. History Through the Eyes of Everyday People* (Alexandria, Va.: Close Up Publishing, 1994), p. 212.

A Physicist's Recollections of the Manhattan Project, 1945: from interview of Philip Morrison in Terkel, *The Good War,* pp. 509–516.

"Japan Surrenders: End of War," *New York Times,* August 15, 1945.

INDEX

DISCARD